English ID

BRITISH ENGLISH EDITION

3
WORKBOOK

PAUL SELIGSON
JOSÉ LUIS MORALES

Richmond

ID Language Map – WB

		Question Syllabus	Vocabulary	Grammar	Speaking / Skill
1	1.1	Do you know all your classmates?		Questions with prepositions	Answer questions about yourself
	1.2	How did your parents meet?	Relationships / Phrasal verbs		Compare love stories
	1.3	How many Facebook friends have you got?	Types of friends	Review of present tenses / Prepositions	Do a quiz about someone you're attracted to
	1.4	When is the right moment to settle down?	Personality adjectives	Emphatic forms	Create your own puzzle
	1.5	How much time do you spend online?	Active listening phrases		Listen & order the story of Antony & Cleopatra
2	2.1	How green are you?	Going green		Answer questions about green habits
	2.2	How long have you been studying here?	Time / Frequency / Degree phrases	Present perfect continuous	
	2.3	Which is worse: flooding or drought?	The environment	Present perfect vs present perfect continuous	Ask & answer about personal habits
	2.4	What's the best advert you've seen recently?		Past simple vs present perfect / continuous	Talk about your work experience
	2.5	Do you support any charities?	Endangered species / Expressions of percentage		Talk about endangered species
3	3.1	Which city would you most like to visit?	Cities	Such / Such a(n)	Describe your hometown
	3.2	Was your weekend as fun as you'd hoped?	Social conventions	Past perfect	Write a review
	3.3	Does the traffic drive you mad?	Urban problems	Past Perfect vs past simple / Conjunctions of contrast	Talk about the problems in your city
	3.4	Have you ever missed any important dates?		Past perfect continuous vs past perfect	
	3.5	How many pets have you owned?	Sign phrases		Listen & make rules
4	4.1	Does your school system work well?	School subjects / Do / Get / Make / Take collocations		Talk about school subjects
	4.2	What's the ideal age to start university?	Career choices / Career advice	Too / Enough / Should / Should not	Talk about school / university life
	4.3	What do you regret not having done?	UK / US differences	Should have + participle	Talk about regrets
	4.4	What would you have said if you'd been late today?	Procrastination	Third conditional	Talk about an embarrassing moment
	4.5	Would you like to be a genius?		A / An / The / Third conditional	Sympathise & criticise
5	5.1	Are you a shopaholic?	Money & shopping / Clothes & accessories	Zero conditional	Share shopping experiences
	5.2	Have you ever borrowed money from a relative?	Loan		Talk about shopping habits
	5.3	Are you a good guesser?		Modals of possibility / probability	Express surprise
	5.4	Have you ever bought a useless product?	Word formation	Order of adjectives	Talk about items you would like to sell
	5.5	Do you often buy things on impulse?	Shopping		

Audio Script p. 54 · Answer Key p. 58 · Phrase Bank p. 64 · Word List p. 70

ID Language Map – WB

		Question Syllabus	Vocabulary	Grammar	Speaking / Skill
6	6.1	Are you addicted to TV?	TV genres & expressions; Compound nouns	Prepositions	Talk about TV preferences
	6.2	What's your favourite TV programme?	Turn phrases	Relative Clauses 1; A / An / The	Ask & answer about TV preferences
	6.3	What were the last three films you saw?		Relative Clauses 2	
	6.4	Where do you usually watch films?		As / Like	Talk about jobs you / your parents have / had in the past
	6.5	When was the last time you did something crazy?		In / On	Answer a quiz
7	7.1	Does technology drive you mad?	Car parts; Phrasal verbs		
	7.2	What was the last little lie you told?	Say vs tell	Reported Speech 1	Talk about the worst lie you've told
	7.3	Are you confident with technology?		Indirect questions	Create questions to ask your country's president
	7.4	Are machines with personality a good idea?		Reported Speech 2	Report requests & commands
	7.5	Do you spend too much time on social networks?	Point phrases	A / The	Share your free time activities
8	8.1	How important are looks?	Appearance	Reflexive pronouns	Record a podcast about your beauty secrets
	8.2	Do you like to hear gossip?		Modal perfects – *must have, can't have, may / might have*	Speculate about people's lives
	8.3	Have you ever cut your own hair?	Have vs get	Causative form	Talk about the things you do & the things you get done
	8.4	Have you got a lot of furniture in your room?	Furniture	Question tags	Describe your bedroom
	8.5	Is your listening improving?	Both / Either; Word formation		Talk about learning a foreign language
9	9.1	Does crime often worry you?	Crime & violence	Review of verb families	Create sentences about crime
	9.2	How could your city be improved quickly?		Passive voice	Talk about what makes you proud of your city
	9.3	Where will you be living in five years' time?	By	Future perfect / continuous	Talk about your plans for next weekend
	9.4	Have you ever been to court?	Crime & punishment	Prepositions	Talk about yourself
	9.5	What was your best birthday present ever?	Excuse phrases		
10	10.1	What makes you angry?	Moods	Binomials	Share your favourite love, hate or anger quote
	10.2	Have you got any pet hates?	Common expressions with *for* & *of*	Gerunds	Talk about a pet hate
	10.3	How assertive are you?		Verb + gerund or infinitive; Tense review	
	10.4	Would you say you were bossy?	Phrasal verbs	Separable & inseparable phrasal verbs; Reflexive pronouns	
	10.5	What's your most common mistake in English?			Talk about your strengths & weaknesses in English

Audio Script p. 56   Answer Key p. 61   Phrase Bank p. 67   Word List p. 71

1

1.1 Do you know all your classmates?

1 Match speed-friending events 1-3 to people a-g.

1 Come to the iD party!
New at the school? Don't worry!
Speed-friending is a great way to meet new people and practise your speaking!
When: Friday, 28th September 8.30pm.
Where: The iD Social Club
First 20 to register get a free snack!
For more info, contact the Students' Social Officer.

2 The Volunteer Society
Speed-friending for people who care
Want to make the world a better place? Come and share ideas with people who feel the same as you.
Monday, 7th December
7.30pm-9.30pm
@Greenton Hall, St. Luke's Street.
Register by emailing bigheart@volunteerone.com.

3 East End Speed-friending and raffle
Come and meet your neighbours in the East End
Wednesday, 5th May
6.00pm-8.00pm
Boone Community Center
Spend a few minutes with each person and get to know them all. Bring some food too; it's a great conversation starter! There will be a raffle at the end of the evening and we have some great prizes!
Contact Mrs Hilary Dunn for more information.

a ☐ I've just moved into the East End.
b ☐ I just hate the silly, superficial small talk typical of speed-friending.
c ☐ I'm a language student and I love parties.
d ☐ I'm free on 28th September.
e ☐ My friends and I do volunteer work for a couple of charities when we can.
f ☐ Cooking is something I'm really good at.
g ☐ It's three weeks to Xmas. I don't want to spend the holidays alone.

2 Order the words in a-g to form questions. Be careful: there's one extra word in each.

a someone / date / on / when / what / you / do / for / look / you / ?
b teachers / last / like / were / what / the / your / year / ?
c at / really / are / what / you / is / good / ?
d something / if / do / what / amazing / could / you / now / one / would / right / be / it / ?
e you / it / what's / without / something / live / can't / just / ?
f out / by / with / would / who / like / you / go / to / ?
g to / closer / family / which / feel / do / does / members / you / ?

3 ▶ 1.1 Match questions a-g from 2 to these answers. Listen to check and add one word to each answer.

☐ My mum and my little brother, I guess.
☐ This colleague I have at the office, no doubt about that.
☐ My mobile phone, for sure.
☐ I'd kiss you. That's if you wanted me to.
☐ Reading and writing. I'm not very good at speaking or listening.
☐ I'd be lying if I didn't say looks.
☐ Cool. Well, most of them.

4 ▶ 1.2 **MAKE IT PERSONAL** Listen to the questions and answer using these words.

first dates   laptop   mum   national park   sport

a What's something you just can't live without?
Well, let's see...

b What are you good at?
That's a difficult one. Er...

c What makes you nervous?
That's a good question. Well...

d Who are you closer to, your mum or your dad?
Hmm, let me think...

e What's the most fun place you've been to?
Hmm, I'm not sure...

⏻ Cyber Tool

Record your answers to the questions in 2 and 4 on www.vocaroo.com and send them to your teacher.

How did your parents meet?

1 Three authors made notes for a love story. Complete the notes with one word in each gap.

Love Story 1
They meet.
They fall _____ love.
They _____ engaged.
They get married.
They drift _____.
They get divorced.

Love Story 2
They met.
They got _____ really well.
They fell _____ each other.
_____ _____ engaged.
They _____ married.
They lived happily ever after.

Love Story 3
They start hanging _____.
She falls _____ him.
They move _____ together.
He'll cheat _____ her.
They'll break _____.
They'll get _____ together.

2 Match the stories in 1 to their views: a, b or c.

a A fairy tale.
b A boomerang relationship.
c An extinguished candle.

3 Read the summary of *Romeo and Juliet*. Number the events in the correct order, 1-9.

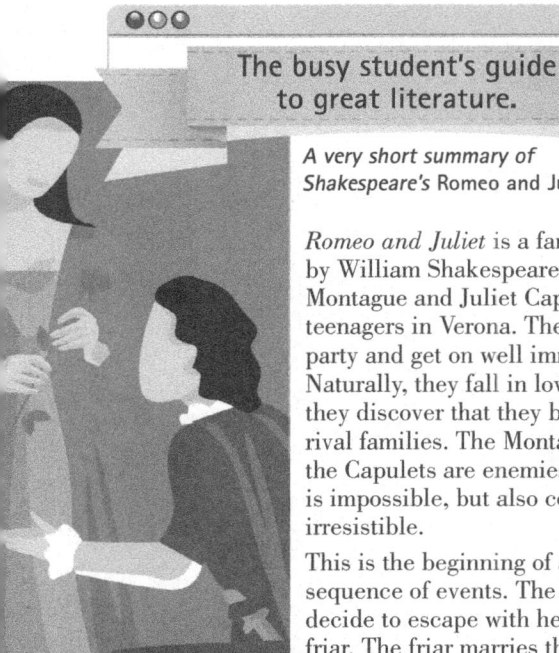

The busy student's guide to great literature.

A very short summary of Shakespeare's Romeo and Juliet.

Romeo and Juliet is a famous play by William Shakespeare. Romeo Montague and Juliet Capulet are teenagers in Verona. They meet at a party and get on well immediately. Naturally, they fall in love, but, later, they discover that they belong to rival families. The Montagues and the Capulets are enemies. Their love is impossible, but also completely irresistible.

This is the beginning of a tragic sequence of events. The lovers decide to escape with help from a friar. The friar marries them secretly, but they can't stay together. Romeo goes back to Verona. The friar has a plan. He gives Juliet a herbal drink. She will 'sleep' for 42 hours, enough for everyone to think she is dead. Then they will get together and leave Verona. Sadly, Romeo hears about Juliet's death, but doesn't know about the plan. He can't live without Juliet. He buys some poison, finds Juliet and kills himself. Juliet wakes up and, finding Romeo dead, she takes his dagger and kills herself too. This classic romance has been an inspiration for generations of authors since.

4 ▶ 1.3 Listen to the summary of *Romeo and Juliet* without reading. Check how much you understood.

☐ 10-20% ☐ 30-50% ☐ 60-80% ☐ 90-100%

Cyber Tool

Find a simple summary of a well-known love story online. Swap links with a study partner and decide which you both prefer. Rate your understanding 10-100% and send the link to your teacher.

5 ▶ 1.4 Look at the sound picture for the schwa, /ə/. Listen and repeat the sound and the words.

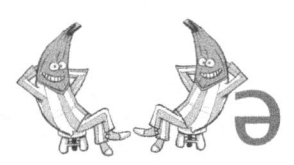

6 ▶ 1.5 Listen to extracts a-d and circle the schwas in each line. The number is in brackets.

a They meet at a party and get on well immediately. (4)
b Their love is impossible but also irresistible. (2)
c The friar marries them secretly. (4)
d ... but they can't stay together. (2)

☐ Romeo dies
☐ escape
☐ meet
☐ Juliet dies
☐ get married secretly
☐ find out their families are enemies
☐ fall for each other
☐ get on well
☐ realise their love is impossible

1.3 How many Facebook friends have you got?

1 ▶1.6 Order the words in italics to complete definitions a-d. Listen to check.

   a Acquaintances generally aren't *can / on / count / people / you /* .
   b Friends are *usually / people / are / in / with / contact / you /* .
   c Good friends are *on / people / get / with / you / and / out / hang / with /* .
   d Very close friends are *always / rely / people / can / on / you / the /* .

2 ▶1.7 Listen to a podcast about International UnFriend Day. What is it?

3 ▶1.7 Listen again. According to the podcast, which two things define a true friend? Someone who…

   ☐ is on your Facebook.
   ☐ helps you move house.
   ☐ shares his / her routine with you.
   ☐ has seen you recently.
   ☐ asks curious questions about you.
   ☐ is very good and nice.

4 Complete the Facebook comments.

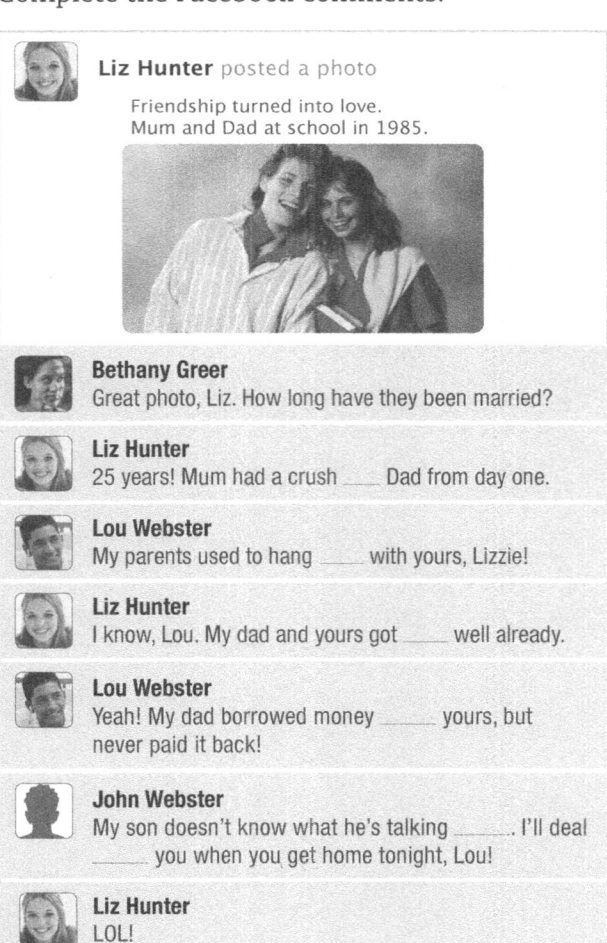

   Liz Hunter posted a photo
   Friendship turned into love.
   Mum and Dad at school in 1985.

   Bethany Greer
   Great photo, Liz. How long have they been married?

   Liz Hunter
   25 years! Mum had a crush _____ Dad from day one.

   Lou Webster
   My parents used to hang _____ with yours, Lizzie!

   Liz Hunter
   I know, Lou. My dad and yours got _____ well already.

   Lou Webster
   Yeah! My dad borrowed money _____ yours, but never paid it back!

   John Webster
   My son doesn't know what he's talking _____ . I'll deal _____ you when you get home tonight, Lou!

   Liz Hunter
   LOL!

5 ▶1.8 Listen to a-f and tick the correct column, acquaintances (A), friends (F) or very close friends (V).

	A	F	V
a Tom and Lucy			
b Ben and Lou			
c J J and Bill			
d Sue and Rob			
e Joe and Pete			
f Meg and Amy			

6 (MAKE IT **PERSONAL**) Think of someone you're attracted to and do the quiz. Write yes (Y) or cross no (N) in the first box.

Will it be love?

   a ☐☐ Does this person give you intense looks?
   b ☐☐ Does he or she often hold your hand or hug you?
   c ☐☐ Have you spent more time together lately?
   d ☐☐ Is your heart beating faster as you answer these questions?
   e ☐☐ Do you spend more time with this person than with other friends?
   f ☐☐ Do you like to talk with this person before you go to sleep every night?
   g ☐☐ Have you and your friend felt jealous of each other lately?
   h ☐☐ Are you going on holiday together any time soon?

   Mostly Yes? Are you already married to this person?
   50 / 50? Try a bit harder; he or she might be interested in you too.
   Mostly No? Give up and find someone else.

7 ▶1.9 Listen to Gwen doing the quiz. Tick / Cross her answers in the second box. What should she do?

8 Classify questions a-h in 6: present simple (PS), present continuous (PC) or present perfect (PP).

Cyber Tool

Search the Internet for more quizzes like this. Which phrase gives you the most appropriate selection: a) friendship into love, b) love your friends or c) lovely friend?

When is the right moment to settle down?

1 What are these people like? Read and complete their profiles with these adjectives.

> adventure-seeking   easygoing
> ~~knowledgeable~~   open-minded   outgoing
> thoughtful   like-minded

Really Desperate Singles

Lena
I'm a <u>serious</u>, <u>knowledgeable</u> PhD student with a <u>love of science and reading</u> who seeks a guy with similar tastes for long-term relationship.

River
Young, _____ biker looks to travel in search of adventure with uncomplicated girl.

Loverboy
_____, funny, friendly, sociable guy is looking for friendly girl to share the simple pleasures of life.

Singlelady
Successful corporate lawyer seeks young, _____ professional who likes to debate and isn't afraid of new ideas.

Freespirit
I am over 40, but I still feel like I'm 18! I'm a fun person with a busy social life. I'm looking for a _____ guy who enjoys nightlife and travel as much as I do.

Gamester
_____ online game champion with no worries looks for similar relaxed girl who loves gaming too.

Joy
Shy, _____ music lover seeks guy with simple tastes for friendship and maybe more.

2 Underline all the words in **1** that helped you choose the right adjectives, as in the example.

> **⏻ Cyber Tool**
> Google 'puzzle maker' and make your own wordsearch with the 12 personality adjectives from lesson 1.4. Share it with your classmates.

3 ▶ 1.10 Complete Nas and Bev's conversation about the people in **1** with emphatic forms of the words in brackets. Listen to check.

Bev So, Lena <u>does seem</u> very smart. (seem)
Nas She certainly does. She's just too knowledgeable for my taste, though. How do you like Gamester?
Bev I _____ to relax, but I'm not crazy about online games. (like)
Nas You certainly aren't.
Bev What about Joy? She _____ pretty. (sure / look)
Nas I _____ music too, but can't imagine myself with a shy girl. (really / love)
Bev You? Shy? No way!
Nas I _____ difficult to please, aren't I? (sure / be)
Bev Absolutely! Well, how about Freespirit? You _____ having fun. (enjoy)
Nas She's over 40, Bev! I _____ too young for her! (definitely / be)

4 ▶ 1.11 Listen and copy the stress and intonation in extracts a-g.

5 Match questions a-e to the opinions.
a What's important to you in a date?
b What do you think about people who date older people?
c Are intelligence and IQ important to you?
d What do you think about online dating?
e Do you agree that opposites attract?

☐ I do believe intelligence is important, but I don't know about IQ.
☐ They sure do, but I definitely think they don't work well in long-term relationships.
☐ I don't know. I've always dated people my age.
☐ A lot of things, but I believe it's important to share the same values.
☐ I do think it's dangerous to date someone you met online.

6 ▶ 1.12 **MAKE IT PERSONAL** Listen to check and email your opinion to your teacher.

1.5 How much time do you spend online?

♪In the car, I just can't wait to pick you up on our very first date.♪

1 People a-j have met through a dating service. Read and decide what each person wants after their first date.

Friendship — Nothing — Love

a Jerry about Wang: 'I had a good time with Wang. We both like *Star Trek* films, but that's not enough for me.'
b Wang about Jerry: 'Jerry's such a charming guy. I hope he'll ask me out again.'
c Zoe about Joe: 'Joe is the most handsome guy I've ever met. He's totally gorgeous!'
d Joe about Zoe: 'Zoe is OK, but I don't know that I'd want to date her.'
e Bernie about Lilly: 'Lilly and I just didn't click at all.'
f Lilly about Bernie: 'Bernie and I didn't get on. Scientific matching isn't perfect after all.'
g Marney about Ben: 'Ben and I had fabulous chemistry for a blind date! He could be the one!'
h Ben about Marney: 'I can't wait to see Marney again. She's such fun, but only as a friend, sadly.'
i Jo about Caleb: 'Well, he is fun to be with, I guess, but there was no attraction between us.'
j Caleb about Jo: 'It was a little embarrassing. She's beautiful, but I don't think she likes me.'

2 ◯ 1.13 Classify bold words in a-h: noun (N), adjective (ADJ), adverb (ADV) or verb (V). Listen and copy the stress and intonation.

a Montagues and Capulets were **rival** families. ADJ
b Romeo and Juliet fell for each other **immediately** when they met. ___
c Romeo and Juliet's was an **impossible** love. ___
d Good **communication** is essential in both friendship and love. ___
e The hardest thing about marriage is learning to **communicate** with each other. ___
f When Jo and I met, there was instant mutual **attraction** between us. ___
g **Respect** is the most important thing in any relationship if it's going to last. ___
h I got a divorce because my ex didn't **respect** me at all. And he was cheating on me too. ___

3 ◯ 1.14 Listen and order the story of Antony and Cleopatra, 1-6.

PRODUCTION: Antony and Cleopatra
SCENE: Caesar and Antony fight to control Egypt. TAKE: ☐

PRODUCTION: Antony and Cleopatra
SCENE: Antony cheats on his wife, Fulvia. TAKE: 1

PRODUCTION: Antony and Cleopatra
SCENE: Antony goes back to Egypt and Cleopatra. TAKE: ☐

PRODUCTION: Antony and Cleopatra
SCENE: Antony marries Caesar's sister, Octavia. TAKE: ☐

PRODUCTION: Antony and Cleopatra
SCENE: Antony and Cleopatra both die. TAKE: ☐

PRODUCTION: Antony and Cleopatra
SCENE: Fulvia dies and Antony goes back to Rome. TAKE: ☐

4 ◯ 1.15 Follow the model. React to the stories you hear.

Model: Antony is married to Flavia.
You: You mean Fulvia, right?

a You mean Fulvia, right?
b No way! With Cleopatra, right?
c So what happens next?
d Hang on a sec! He marries Caesar's sister?
e Are you serious? He cheats on her too?
f And then?
g Whoa! What a crazy story!

5 Find the connection between the song line above and this lesson. Do the same with the other four song lines in unit 1 of the Student's Book.

Can you remember...
▸ 6 questions ending with prepositions? SB → p. 5
▸ 6 phrases to think a little before you answer? SB → p. 5
▸ 7 phrasal verbs for relationships? SB → p. 7
▸ 3 verb forms for the present? SB → p. 9
▸ 3 English nouns that became cyber verbs? SB → p. 9
▸ 6 compound adjectives for personality? SB → p. 10
▸ when auxiliary verbs are stressed? SB → p. 11

How green are you?

2.1

1 Read the start of the article and tick the correct meaning of 'go off the grid'.
- [ ] not use regular electricity
- [ ] ride a bike (cycle)
- [ ] switch the lights off

Pedal! For how long?

Physics teacher John Cornell's classroom at Henleigh High School will 'go off the grid' for a day this Friday. But that does not mean they can't use any electrical items. Instead, there'll be pedal power to generate electricity.

2 Read the rest of the article. True (T) or false (F)? Correct the false statements.

Cornell and another teacher connected a bike to a power generator two weeks ago. As students pedal, their energy is converted into electricity that is stored in a car battery in the classroom.

'Students have been coming into our classroom an hour before lessons and staying for another hour after school to power the generator by cycling', Cornell said. When the battery's full, the students will vote for what they want to use the electricity for. Students will then calculate how much energy they'll need to do whatever they want to do.

For example, to watch a film, they'll need to cycle for 72 minutes in order to power the TV and DVD player. To make waffles, they'll need much more energy and more pedalling. 'This project is great fun and we've learned a lot', a student commented. 'To get electricity you have to do hard work. I unplug my laptop and mobile phone charger when I'm not using them now', another confirmed.

a Cornell is a chemistry teacher who started this idea on his own.
b The generator and battery are in different rooms.
c Students have been generating electricity on their own time.
d The teacher tells them how much energy each item needs.
e Watching a film in lessons uses more energy than powering a waffle maker.
f At least one of John's students has learned to be greener.

3 Add one word to complete comments a-g. Are the speakers green (G) or not green (NG)?

a Yeah! We won't use plastic cups in this office anymore.
b What? Three thousand pounds for couple of solar panels? Forget it!
c Can have a couple more plastic bags, please?
d It's pretty simple be eco-friendly. I just try to reuse, reduce and recycle.
e What? Recycling? It's useless. Forget!
f Are you joking? Why take the stairs when you can take lift?
g I work in same office as my neighbour, Bill. Sometimes he drives me; other days I drive him.

4 ▶ 2.1 Match a-g in 3 to the replies. Listen to check.
- [ ] Yes, but you will save a lot more money than that on electricity bills.
- [ ] I'm so glad. Those cups take 500 years to decompose.
- [ ] I know. The three Rs. But it's not so easy!
- [ ] No, it isn't. Think of all the rubbish you create when you throw things away.
- [ ] Can I join you? That'd make it cheaper for the three of us.
- [ ] Because the exercise is good for you and it will save energy.
- [ ] Here you are. Would you like to buy a reusable bag?

5 Order the words to form green survey questions.

a plastic / home / you / do / recycle / at / ?
   Do you recycle plastic at home?
b clothes / do / buy / used / you / any / ?
c you / have / home / energy-efficient / light bulbs / do / at / ?
d transport / using / of / you / to / walked / have / or / cycled / work / lately / instead / private / ?
e when / appliances / using / you're / you / do / switch off / not / them / ?
f use / do / you / eco-friendly / products / cleaning / ?
g have / plastic / reusable / changed / from / you / to / cloth bags / ?

Cyber Tool

Record your answers to the questions a-g on www.vocaroo.com and share them with a classmate.

6 ▶ 2.2 Match a-d to the responses. Find four examples of /ɒ/ or /əʊ/ in each pair. Listen to check.

/ɒ/　　　　　　　/əʊ/

a Is the hotel down the road open?
b Don't go on your own. I'll come with you.
c Has John gone to the vet?
d Hey, that's a nice top!

- [ ] Yeah. His dog stopped eating.
- [ ] Thanks a lot. I got it at the new shop.
- [ ] I'll phone and ask them.
- [ ] Great! Get your coat.

2.2 How long have you been studying here?

1 Amir made a list of 'green' resolutions on 1st January. Use the notes to complete his blog with the present perfect continuous ⊕ or ⊖. There is one extra note.

Notes

Resolutions for a greener New Year
- Cycle more often.
- Do not buy disposable products.
- Separate the rubbish.
- Replace appliances with energy-efficient ones.
- Buy more eco-friendly products.
- Don't take taxis.

posts | about | contact

🍃 30th June

I've been trying to go green for the last six months. It hasn't been easy, but I feel truly proud of myself. So far I've managed to change quite a few things for the better. So, first of all <u>I've been cycling</u> to work twice a week. The exercise is good for me and I feel a lot healthier now, but it isn't much fun when it's windy and worse when it rains! ☹ And also on transport, _____. It makes it hard to get home at night, but I'm saving a lot of money.

At home _____, you know, the organic from the non-biodegradable waste. It's kind of disgusting at times, but my rubbish bin's a lot emptier now.

Actually, dealing with the rubbish is easier now because _____ like polystyrene cups and aluminium cans. And another thing, _____ to use around the house, like cleaning products. They are as good as the old ones, but they are a little more expensive. Even my shampoo is eco-friendly, and you know what? My hair looks great!

2 Re-read and answer a-f.

a How does Amir feel about his achievement?
b What's the disadvantage of cycling to work?
c What's the advantage of not taking taxis?
d Does Amir enjoy separating the rubbish?
e Are eco-friendly products similar to the old ones?
f Does Amir's blog encourage you to do the same?

3 ▶ 2.3 Many countries have been going green lately. Read changes a-h and predict which country is doing each. Listen to check.

<u>Austria</u> Brazil Costa Rica France
Iceland Norway Sweden Switzerland

GRADUALLY GETTING GREENER?

a In <u>Austria</u>, architects have been building energy-efficient houses.
b _____ has been using clean electricity from geothermal energy.
c _____ has been building national Alpine parks.
d _____ has been planting millions of trees to reduce deforestation.
e _____ has been using more water and wind power for electricity.
f _____ has been collaborating with Sweden to produce clean energy.
g _____ has been producing a lot of its fuel from sugar cane.
h In _____, more families have been installing solar panels at home.

4 Correct two mistakes in each of a-g.

a The office have been really busy. We've been worked like mad.
b I like your shoes. I've been trying find a pair like that last year.
c So sorry! Have you been waited for a long?
d Hey! I've been trying to phone you yesterday. Where was you?
e He's been studied English for year.
f They've been playing the football before.
g Joan been managing the company advertising since 2012.

5 ▶ 2.4 Make sentences with the present perfect continuous. Follow the model.

Model: Try to ring you.
You: I've been trying to ring you.

Which is worse: flooding or drought?

2.3

1 Order the letters in 'environment' phrases a-i.

a NGIAOPCH
b RDUGOHTS
c OSLDFO
d NSEDROFATOIET
e NGIRSI ESA VLEESL
f PNGIUDM FO EESTWA
g TNHERTDEAE PCEISES
h LFSOSI LSEFU
i LGBOLA GNIRAWM

2 ▶2.5 Listen to two students and tick the four problems in 1 they mention.

3 ▶2.5 Listen again and answer a-f.
 a Does their city suffer from floods or droughts?
 b Were Lucy and Mikaela personally affected?
 c Have the authorities repaired all of the damage?
 d When was the last time it rained in the north?
 e What percentage of the Earth is water?
 f Which country does Lucy give as an example?

Cyber Tool
Choose the three most serious problems in 1, globally or locally. Text your choices to a friend. Any differences?

4 ▶2.6 Imagine significant progress is made in the next 50 years to protect the environment. Read the future news and write the verbs in the present perfect or perfect continuous. Listen to check.

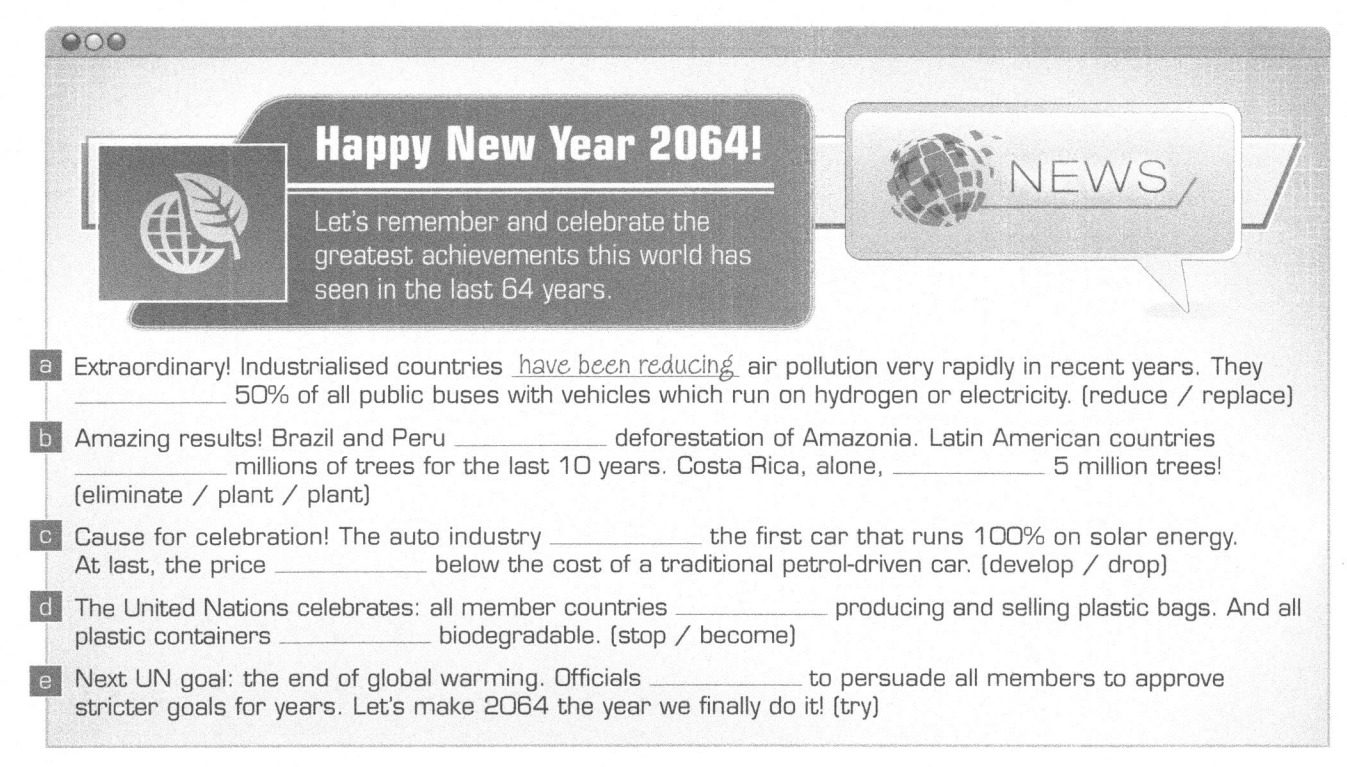

Happy New Year 2064!
Let's remember and celebrate the greatest achievements this world has seen in the last 64 years.

NEWS

a Extraordinary! Industrialised countries _have been reducing_ air pollution very rapidly in recent years. They _____ 50% of all public buses with vehicles which run on hydrogen or electricity. (reduce / replace)

b Amazing results! Brazil and Peru _____ deforestation of Amazonia. Latin American countries _____ millions of trees for the last 10 years. Costa Rica, alone, _____ 5 million trees! (eliminate / plant / plant)

c Cause for celebration! The auto industry _____ the first car that runs 100% on solar energy. At last, the price _____ below the cost of a traditional petrol-driven car. (develop / drop)

d The United Nations celebrates: all member countries _____ producing and selling plastic bags. And all plastic containers _____ biodegradable. (stop / become)

e Next UN goal: the end of global warming. Officials _____ to persuade all members to approve stricter goals for years. Let's make 2064 the year we finally do it! (try)

5 ▶2.7 Write present perfect questions a-h. Use the continuous form where possible. Listen, check and write the answers you hear.
 a How long / you / know / your best friend?
 b You / work hard / recently?
 c You / ever / live / in a different city?
 d How long / you / study / today?
 e How much bread / you / eat / today?
 f How far / you / walk / today?
 g How many cups of coffee / you / drink / today?
 h You / exercise / a lot / lately?

Cyber Tool
Record and send your answers to a classmate. Any surprises?

2.4 What's the best advert you've seen recently?

1 Read and match pop-up adverts 1-5 to Internet users a-e.

a I'm a qualified young woman with no previous experience. I need to get a job fast.
b We're football fans and we're tired of adverts on TV.
c I'm a senior manager working for a multinational company. I am looking for an agent who can help me manage my career.
d I'm a sales representative for a large consumer goods company that hopes to export to Asian countries.
e I'm a Mac user with a slow, slow laptop. Get me out of here!

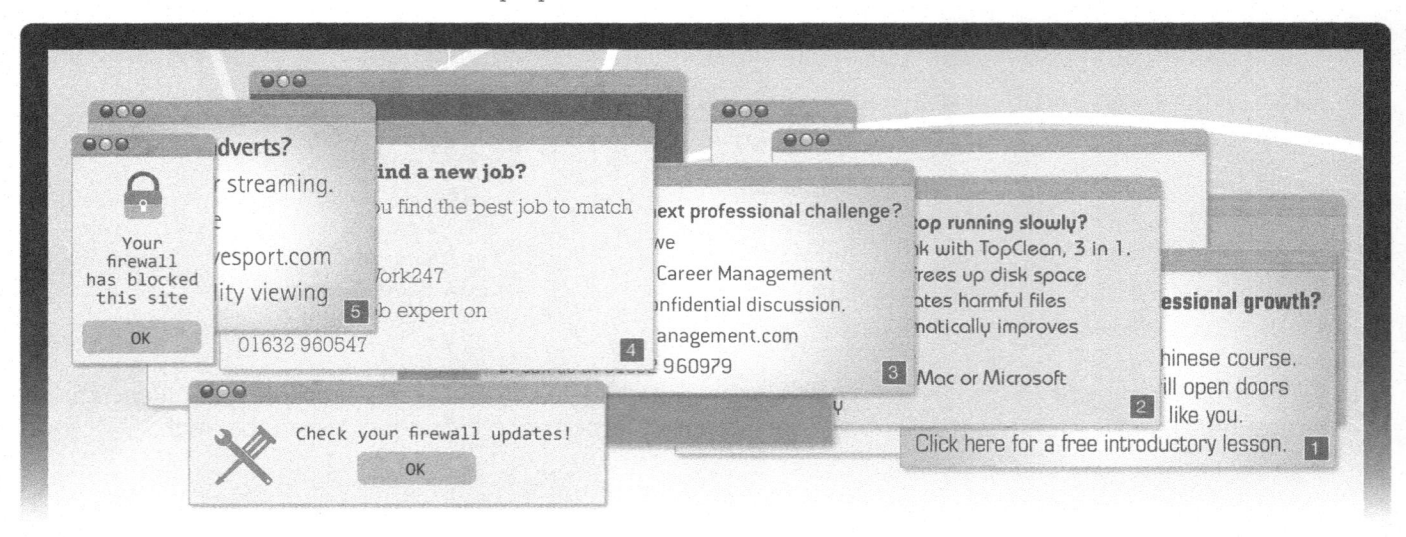

2 ▶2.8 (MAKE IT **PERSONAL**) Predict and write the words you can't see. Listen to check. Would you contact any of these companies?

3 Add the missing words to make full questions.

a Ready for professional growth?
b Laptop running slowly?
c Looking for your next professional challenge?
d Want to find a new job?
e Tired of adverts?

4 ▶2.9 Listen to three calls to the companies in 1 and answer a-f. Mia (M), Cal (C) or Jake (J)?
Which caller...
a has not contacted the company before?
b has never met a representative of the company before?
c has been waiting the longest?
d received a guarantee?
e leaves contact details?
f currently has no work?

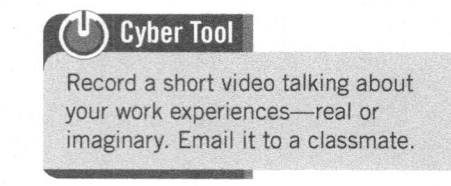

> **Cyber Tool**
> Record a short video talking about your work experiences—real or imaginary. Email it to a classmate.

5 ▶2.9 Complete extracts a-f with the correct form of the verbs in brackets. Listen again to check.

a I _____ in for an interview a couple of weeks ago. (come)
b It _____ two weeks and I _____ anything from you. (be / not hear)
c Hello. You _____ the offices of Grabowsky and Loewe. (reach)
d I _____ in the oil industry for 17 years now. (work)
e I _____ a copy of *Selling in China for Beginners* and, er, it _____ yet. (order / not arrive)
f I _____ my bank account and I _____ five weeks ago, so I _____ for 35 days. (check / pay / wait)

Do you support any charities?

♪ Now I'm floating like a butterfly. Stinging like a bee I earned my stripes. ♪   **2.5**

1 ▶ 2.10 Listen to four dialogues and identify the animals mentioned in each.

> Giant panda   Golden lion tamarin   Hawaiian monk seal
> Ivory-billed woodpecker   Javanese rhino   Mountain gorilla   Northern right whale

2 ▶ 2.11 These extracts are in phonetics. Can you decipher them? Listen to check and notice the /ə/.
  a /aɪm gəʊɪŋ tə teɪk ə fəʊtəgrɑːf/
  b /aɪ kən siː ðæt ðeɪ ə(r) iːtɪŋ fruːt/
  c /hələʊ ənd welkəm tə zuː ətlæntə/
  d /mʌðə(r) ənd tʃaɪld trævəlɪŋ ələʊŋ/

3 ▶ 2.12 (MAKE IT **PERSONAL**) Order the words in a-e to form questions. Cross out the extra word in each. Listen, check and answer.
  a animal / you / have / ever / endangered / a / seen / an / in / wild / the / ?
  b a / you / have / a / ever / one / seen / in / zoo / ?
  c animal / sick / looked / on / have / after / you / ever / a / ?
  d given / never / have / you / an / money / for / animal / ever / cause / ?
  e NGO / an / have / ever / considered / you / it / working / for / animal / protection / ?

> **Cyber Tool**
> Which one would you adopt (i.e. give money to a charity to save)? Why? Record your answer and email it to a classmate.

4 Read the charity advert and change the underlined expressions to a percentage (%).

> 🦋 The number of butterflies fell by <u>a fifth</u> in the UK in 2011.
>
> 🦋 The UK's population of small birds went up by <u>a third</u>.
>
> 🦋 There has been <u>hardly any</u> change in the size of the UK's forests over the last 30 years.

5 ▶ 2.13 **Dictation.** Listen and complete a-e with four or five words each. Mark them encouragement (E) or discouragement (D).
  a _____ you'll get there.
  b _____ doing that?
  c Keep going. You'll _____.
  d _____ succeed, try, try again.
  e Do you really think _____?

6 ▶ 2.14 Listen to two short dialogues and tick the phrases in 5 that you hear. What does each person want to do?

7 Find the connection between the song line above and this lesson. Do the same with the other four song lines in unit 2 of the Student's Book.

Can you remember...
- 7 'green' adjectives using -able, -efficient and -friendly? SB → p.15
- 3 words that rhyme with *go* and 3 that rhyme with *hot*? SB → p.15
- 4 frequency expressions, 4 quantity expressions and 8 time expressions? SB → p.17
- 9 environmental disasters / problems? SB → p.18
- 2 differences between the present perfect and the present perfect continuous? SB → p.19
- 7 species of animals we may never see again? SB → p.22
- 3 encouragement and 3 discouragement expressions? SB → p.23

3

3.1 Which city would you most like to visit?

1 Use the clues to complete the crossword with places of interest in cities.

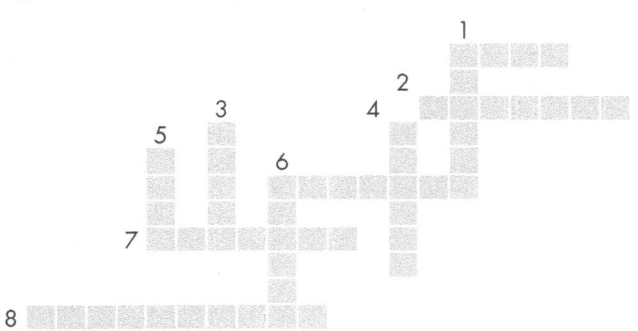

Across:
1. London was once famous for its thick grey ___.
2. Sydney ___ is famous for its iconic Opera House and magnificent bridge.
6. You can see the city's ___ from the observation deck at the top of the Empire State building.
7. The Louvre and the Smithsonian are some of the most-visited ___ in the world.
8. How many floors has the highest ___ in the world got?

Down:
1. The ___ of Liberty is one of New York City's most famous landmarks.
3. Well-planned cities usually have some ___. We all need and enjoy these green spaces.
4. San Francisco's Golden Gate ___ is a famous red landmark.
5. There are crowded ___ in or around most big cities in the world. Many of them are dangerous.
6. Every city has a main ___. There are usually impressive buildings around it.

2 ▶ 3.1 Order the words in a-d. Complete the answers with *a* or *the*. Listen to check. What city is it?

a you / like / city / how / your / do / ?
   It's _____ truly awesome city; _____ city that never sleeps; _____ capital of _____ world.

b way / it / easy / is / to / your / around / find / ?
   It is really easy to find your way around because _____ streets are numbered.

c your / what's / landmark / favourite / ?
   Well, in _____ city of skyscrapers, I guess it's _____ Chrysler Building.

d spots / are / the / what / most / tourist / popular / ?
   Central Park, Greenwich Village, 5th Avenue, _____ World Trade Center, and so many others.

3 ▶ 3.2 **MAKE IT PERSONAL** Listen to questions a-d in 2 again and give your own answers about your hometown.

Cyber Tool
Record your answers on www.vocaroo.com and send them to your teacher.

4 Circle the correct option in tweets a-e.

a St Petersburg at last. **Such / Such a** beautiful city!

b We've had **such a / such** delicious fish in Peru!

c Just arrived in sunny Seville. The old city centre has **such / such an** amazing streets!

d The Hong Kong skyline. What a place! **Such an / Such** exceptionally beautiful view!

e Dubai rocks! **Such / Such a** cool architecture everywhere! And the nightlife...!

5 ▶ 3.3 Listen and repeat. Pronounce the underlined sounds correctly.

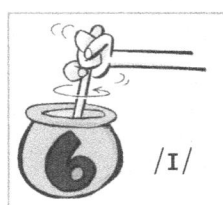

/ɪ/ It's a p<u>i</u>ty our pr<u>e</u>tty c<u>i</u>ty <u>i</u>s now l<u>i</u>ttered w<u>i</u>th l<u>i</u>ttle b<u>i</u>ts of plast<u>i</u>c.

/iː/ Thr<u>ee</u> sl<u>ee</u>py sh<u>ee</u>p on a b<u>ea</u>ch, <u>ea</u>ch <u>ea</u>ting a p<u>ie</u>ce of gr<u>ee</u>n ch<u>ee</u>se.

Was your weekend as fun as you'd hoped? 3.2

1 Chris is in Mumbai to meet his fiancée's family. He's arranged to meet a friend, Roni, first. Read Roni's texts and mark a-f true (T), false (F) or not mentioned (N).

> Finally made it to the hotel, but you'd left. Sorry! Good luck with your in-laws. R
> Sent 17:31

> Remember not to kiss your girlfriend in front of her parents. Terrible manners in India! R
> Sent 17:35

> Almost forgot. Hug her brothers if you want to, but don't kiss them on the cheek, OK? R
> Sent 17:42

> One more: don't greet servants as you do with the family. Just nod. Can u reply, pls? R
> Sent 17:45

> Aha! Can't see my texts 'cause u switched off your mobile as I told you. ☹ R
> Sent 18:36

a By the time Roni got to the hotel, Chris had gone.
b Chris sent five texts to Roni.
c Roni had told Chris to switch his phone off while visiting his future in-laws.
d Chris didn't text Roni back because his mobile phone was off.
e Indian men don't greet other men with kisses.
f You're not supposed to shake hands with the servants.

2 Complete Chris' email to his family with the past perfect form of these verbs.

| break | (not) hug | kiss | make |
| mistake | send | shake | tell |

Dear Mum and Dad,
Greetings from a really rainy Mumbai—I thought it'd be hot and dry. Last night I met Diya's parents. After a tense couple of hours I got back to the hotel, turned my mobile phone back on (Roni _____(a) me to switch it off) and found several text messages with advice from Roni. Too late! He _____(b) those messages while my phone was off. As I read them I realised I _____(c) so many terrible mistakes at Diya's. To begin with, I had kissed her in front of her parents, apparently a big no-no in India. To make matters worse, I _____(d) her brothers too—males usually don't. Worse still, I _____(e) them as you're supposed to. Worst of all, I _____(f) one of the servants for a member of the family and _____(g) hands with her. In India, you greet people from different social backgrounds differently. In other words, I discovered I _____(h) practically every cultural rule in the book.
I just hope they'll give me another chance. Wish me luck! I'll write again soon. Hope Dad's feeling a little better now.
Love,
Chris xx

3 Correct one mistake in each of a-e.
a Did you know the Romans had spoken Latin?
b After we had arrived home, we made some sandwiches.
c By the time we got home, the TV show finished.
d When I had lunch, I had a short nap.
e We had bought our car five years ago.

4 Choose the correct past participle.
a Chris had **been** / **gone** by the time Roni arrived.
b Chris had never **been** / **gone** to Mumbai before.
c Roni had **been** / **gone** to India several times.
d By the time Chris saw Roni's messages, he'd already **been** / **gone** to his in-laws'.

5 ▶ 3.4 Watch / Listen to the guide and circle the word(s) with the strongest stress in a-f. The number of stressed words is in brackets.

a Hi, this is your travel host, Naomi. (4)
b I'd like to show you the top ten attractions of Madrid, Spain. (8)
c Number ten, Plaza de Cibeles. Madrid is known for many beautiful squares like this one. (9)
d The Cibeles fountain is an important symbol of this city. (5)
e Number nine. Almudena Cathedral. It took more than a hundred years to complete its construction in 1993. (8)
f The original site was occupied by Madrid's first mosque. (6)

6 ▶ 3.5 Listen and copy the sentence stress.

Cyber Tool

Go to www.tripadvisor.com and read the reviews for a hotel, restaurant or attraction you know well. Write a short review and share it with a friend.

3.3 Does the traffic drive you mad?

1 ▶ 3.6 Complete Jade's monologue with the correct form of the verbs. Use the past perfect where possible. Listen to check. What city is it?

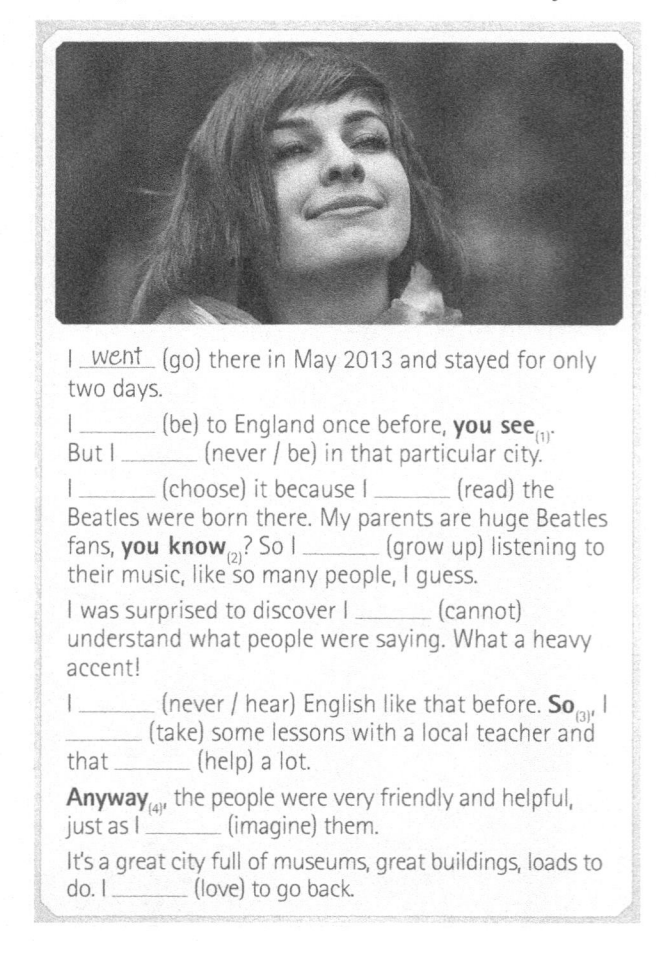

I __went__ (go) there in May 2013 and stayed for only two days.

I _____ (be) to England once before, **you see**(1). But I _____ (never / be) in that particular city.

I _____ (choose) it because I _____ (read) the Beatles were born there. My parents are huge Beatles fans, **you know**(2)? So I _____ (grow up) listening to their music, like so many people, I guess.

I was surprised to discover I _____ (cannot) understand what people were saying. What a heavy accent!

I _____ (never / hear) English like that before. **So**(3), I _____ (take) some lessons with a local teacher and that _____ (help) a lot.

Anyway(4), the people were very friendly and helpful, just as I _____ (imagine) them.

It's a great city full of museums, great buildings, loads to do. I _____ (love) to go back.

2 Match the **bold** expressions in 1 to their use.

To return to your story. ☐☐
To check your listener understands what you mean. ☐☐

Cyber Tool

Record a similar monologue about a place you've been to. Send it to a classmate who has to guess which city it is.

3 ▶ 3.7 Listen to Spiros and write loves (L), hates (H) or not a problem (N).

a People who don't respect traffic signs.
b People who honk.
c Littering.
d Traffic fumes.
e Potholes.
f Roadworks.
g Heavy traffic.
h Traffic police.
i Thieves.

4 Read Spiros' blog. Circle the correct word(s).

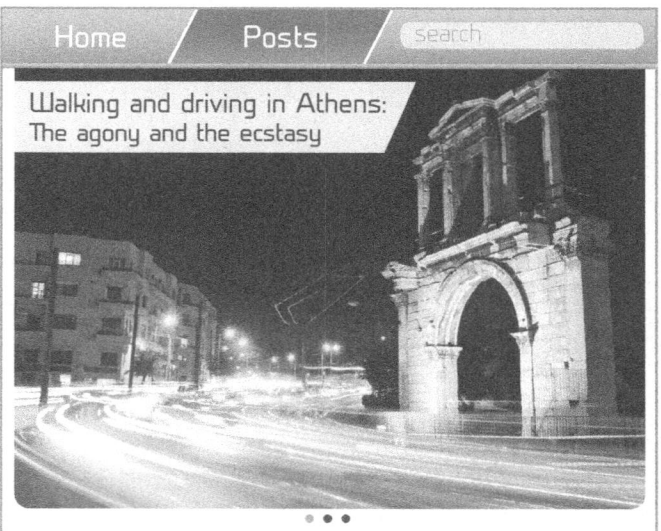

Walking and driving in Athens: The agony and the ecstasy

It's a real privilege to live in a city that has some of the world's oldest, most amazing buildings. There are many things I love about my city. But it's not all roses, **though / even though**(a). For a start, **in spite / although**(b) most big cities in the world have heavy traffic, in Athens it is particularly bad. The air is often very dirty and traffic fumes are damaging the beautiful buildings our city is famous for.

Drivers generally complain about traffic and traffic police, for example. I think they do a great job, **although / though**(c). People who don't respect traffic signs can cause serious accidents and something should be done about it. So, **although / however**(d) honking isn't pleasant, I find drivers going through red lights and driving in the bus lane far worse.

Drivers and pedestrians alike complain about potholes and roadworks in our city. I think you can't have it all. **Even though / However**(e) roadworks can be a nuisance, it is a sign that something is being done to fix some of the problems we all complain about.

5 (MAKE IT **PERSONAL**) Complete sentences a-c. Use the ideas from the box to help you. Text your answers to a friend.

| honking littering parking space |
| pothole red light thieves traffic jam |

a I don't mind _____, but _____ really annoys me.
b I wouldn't live in a city where _____.
c In big cities, it's difficult to _____.

Have you ever missed any important dates?   3.4

1 Match tweets a-e to the places they'd been. There are two extra places.
   - [ ] out to eat
   - [ ] to a football match
   - [ ] to a pop concert
   - [ ] to the cinema
   - [ ] to the opera
   - [ ] to the park
   - [ ] to the theatre

a **Lisa** — No voice left after singing along to Jessie J. Wow! She's awesome!

b **Diego** — Yawn! That was the most boring play I've ever seen.

c **Jamilah** — Yum yum! Best meal I've had in a long time. Luv ya Dad!

d **Lucy** — Not in the mood for Adam Sandler. Left halfway through it.

e **Jake** — Just saying. Arsenal could have done better.

2 ▶ 3.8 Listen to problems a-g and match them to these sentences.
   - [ ] He'd been locked out of the house.
   - [a] He'd been stuck in a traffic jam.
   - [ ] They'd been stuck in an underground train.
   - [ ] They'd been stuck in a lift.
   - [ ] They'd been locked out of their car.
   - [ ] They'd been stuck at the top of a building.
   - [ ] They'd been stuck in a queue for hours.

3 ▶ 3.9 What had they been doing? Listen, choose the correct verb and write your guesses below.

   | dance | do exercise | fight | fly | speed |

   a Bill and Jim _____.
   b Meg and her boyfriend _____.
   c Betty and Pete _____.
   d Joe and his girlfriend _____.
   e Suki _____.

4 Complete a-e with the verbs in brackets in the past perfect or past perfect continuous.

   a Marge watched her husband come in and collapse on the settee. He _____ with his friends in the bar. (hang out)

   b As he walked through the door, he knew Wilma _____ his favourite brontosaurus rib pie. (make)

   c When Stan reached the top of the hill, he realised his friend _____ there a few minutes before. (get)

   d He was almost sick when he found out his roommate Leonard and his neighbour Penny _____ secretly for some time. (date)

   e In the end we find out that Severus Snape _____ Albus Dumbledore. (kill)

5 Two of sentences a-g are correct; the others have one mistake each. Correct them.
   a I had to sit down because I'd stood all day.
   b We got lost because we hadn't been understanding the directions.
   c Julio failed the exam because he hadn't studied enough.
   d Vera had been visiting Turkey before so she knew the best places.
   e Until yesterday night, I'd never been having wine before.
   f Luigi only got married because he'd been living with his mother for 40 years.
   g How long were you waiting when the doors opened?

3.5 How many pets have you owned?

♪All for freedom and for pleasure. Nothing ever lasts forever. Everybody wants to rule the world.♪

1 Order the letters to find the message.

```
O N   E C A R S M A
N O
1 2   3 4 5 6 7 8 9

N I   E H T
        
10 11  12 13 14

I D I B U L N G
15 16 17 18 19 20 21 22
```

2 Use the numbers in 1 to discover the mystery signs a-d. Which one is meant to be funny?

a ST2P 10N T13E N4M14 2F 18OV6.

b R14STR10CTED 4RE8 P7IVA12E P7OPE7TY.

c 19O 21OT 6NT6R, D10VE O7 JU5P.

d 19O NO12 T4LK T2O MU3H. LE12 H14R 19RIV6

3 Match the sign phrases a-g and complete with prepositions.

a Danger! No
b Kindly refrain
c Park here
d Please clean
e Tow
f Vehicles will be

____ after your pet.
____ zone. Do not stop here.
towed ____ owner's expense.
____ your own risk.
lifeguard ____ duty.
____ smoking.

4 ▶ 3.10 Listen to the sound effects and make rules with **can't** after the beep. Follow the model.

Excuse me. I'm afraid you can't take photos here.

5 ▶ 3.11 Match the quotes. Listen to check. Tick your favourite.

a The golden rule is
b Life is short. Break the rules. Forgive quickly. Kiss slowly.
c Know the rules well,
d If you obey all the rules,
e You have to learn the rules of the game.
f There are three rules for writing a novel.

☐ Unfortunately no one knows what they are. Somerset Maugham
☐ so you can break them effectively. Dalai Lama XIV
☐ And then you have to play better than anyone else. Albert Einstein
☐ that there are no golden rules. George Bernard Shaw
☐ you miss all the fun. Katharine Hepburn
☐ Laugh uncontrollably. And never regret anything that makes you smile. Mark Twain

6 How does the song line on this page connect with the language of this lesson? Find the connection between the lessons and song lines in the Student's book for this unit.

Can you remember...

- 7 words for features of a city? SB → p. 26
- 9 customs in Hong Kong? SB → p. 28
- how to use the past perfect? SB → p. 29
- 10 urban problems? SB → p. 30
- the use of *although / (even) though*? SB → p. 31
- 5 phrases to show you are listening? SB → p. 32
- the difference between past perfect and past perfect continuous? SB → p. 33
- the opposite of *arrive on time for an appointment*? SB → p. 33
- 2 people, 4 verbs and 4 preposition phrases from signs? SB → p. 34

Does your school system work well?

1 Add vowels to the school subjects. Circle three /dʒ/ sounds and underline one /tʃ/.

L	T	R	T	R		
	R	T				
G		G	R		P	H	Y
M		T	H	S		
H		S	T		R	Y
L		N	G		G		S
C	H		M		S	T	R	Y
P	H	Y	S		C	S
B		L		G	Y

2 ▶4.1 Listen to two teachers. Who said it? Ruth (R) or Dan (D)?

a I think schools need to teach 21st century skills.
b I believe we should concentrate on reading, writing and arithmetic.
c I think children have to learn how to solve problems creatively.
d In my opinion, smartphones can be a useful learning tool in class.
e Smartphones shouldn't be allowed in class.
f I don't think students should look for information online. It's useless.
g Teachers should teach students to find information on the Internet that they can trust.

3 ▶4.2 Listen and match a–g in 2 to the agree / disagree responses.

Agree	Disagree
I think so too.	I don't think so.
I completely agree with you.	I don't agree with you.
Yeah, you're right.	Oh, come on!

4 ▶4.3 Listen to the sentence stress. Then follow the model.

● ● ● ●
Model: I think so too.
You: I think so too.

5 Complete the mind maps with these words.

> badly   a difference
> an examination   an exercise
> feedback   good marks   homework
> into trouble   kicked out   mistakes
> photos   progress   a report
> a test   well

Do

Get

Make

Take

6 Match the sentences a–g. Underline the phrases you don't use much in English.

a I haven't done
b I'm under a lot of pressure to pass
c Who would have guessed I'd get kicked
d I know I should get a
e The only way to do
f It's really no secret that I must get
g The careers adviser told me it takes

☐ degree if I want to get a decent job.
☐ out of school for cheating in a test.
☐ excellent results if I want to get a scholarship.
☐ over five years to train to be a vet.
☐ as well as I expected in school this year.
☐ my exams so I can get into uni.
☐ well at school is to do homework and revise for tests.

Cyber Tool

Which subjects are / were you best / worst at? Why? Record and email it to a classmate.

4.2 What's the ideal age to start university?

1 Read a teacher's social network updates and circle the correct choice.

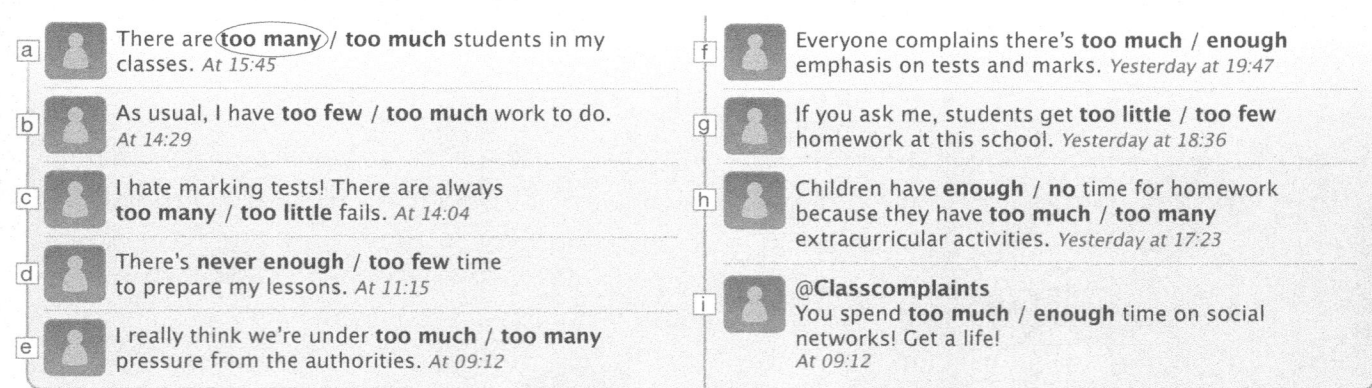

a There are **too many** / **too much** students in my classes. *At 15:45*

b As usual, I have **too few** / **too much** work to do. *At 14:29*

c I hate marking tests! There are always **too many** / **too little** fails. *At 14:04*

d There's **never enough** / **too few** time to prepare my lessons. *At 11:15*

e I really think we're under **too much** / **too many** pressure from the authorities. *At 09:12*

f Everyone complains there's **too much** / **enough** emphasis on tests and marks. *Yesterday at 19:47*

g If you ask me, students get **too little** / **too few** homework at this school. *Yesterday at 18:36*

h Children have **enough** / **no** time for homework because they have **too much** / **too many** extracurricular activities. *Yesterday at 17:23*

i @Classcomplaints You spend **too much** / **enough** time on social networks! Get a life! *At 09:12*

2 Cross out the wrong option in a–c.
  a I haven't got enough **energy** / **money** / **rich** / **time** to…
  b I've got too much **work** / **pressure** / **problems** / **stress** from…
  c There are too many **distractions** / **noise** / **people** / **rules** at…

> **Cyber Tool**
> Record yourself making as many true sentences as you can from a–c and email it to a classmate. Any big differences?

3 What should / shouldn't they do? Read and match career choices to career advice a–f.

Career Choices
- **Lena:** My dad's always wanted me to get into medical school. He'll be terribly disappointed if I don't.
- **Nila:** All my friends are choosing business degrees, so I guess I'll do that too.
- **Melinda:** Three years at university? No way! I have no patience for that.
- **Bob:** I've been on this course for two years. I can't just drop out and start all over again.
- **Jana:** I love languages, but the best jobs always go to business graduates.
- **Jud:** Apply to the Royal Academy of Dramatic Art? There's no way I'll ever get into RADA, man.

Career Advice
a You have to follow your heart, not your head.
b Do what you want, not what everybody else is doing.
c Don't be afraid to fail.
d Never try to live someone else's dream.
e You need to think about your future.
f You mustn't be afraid to make big changes.

4 ▶ 4.4 Listen to the people in 3 and give appropriate career advice using **should** or **shouldn't**. Follow the model.
'My dad's always wanted me to get into medical school. He'll be terribly disappointed if I don't.'
Model: Live someone else's dream.
You: You shouldn't live someone else's dream.

5 ▶ 4.5 Listen and cross out three words that don't match the sound pictures.

| c**ou**ld | f**oo**d | f**u**ture |
| m**u**ch | p**u**t | w**o**man |

6 ▶ 4.6 Listen and repeat a and b. How fast can you go? Be careful to pronounce the /ʊ/ correctly every time.
  a The woman could cook because she read the book.
  b Hey! Look where you're putting your foot!

7 ▶ 4.7 Listen to a joke and circle the words you hear.

Three language students are **talking outside** / **walking to school** for their listening class.
'It's **Wednesday** / **windy**', says Yolanda.
'No, it isn't, it's **Thursday** / **thirsty**', says Jaime.
'Me too,' says Petra, 'Forget class, let's find **a café** / **a coffee**!'

> **Cyber Tool**
> Google 'tongue twisters,' choose one and record yourself saying it.

What do you regret not having done?

1 Is the underlined word American (US) or British (UK)? Write the other option too. Follow the example.

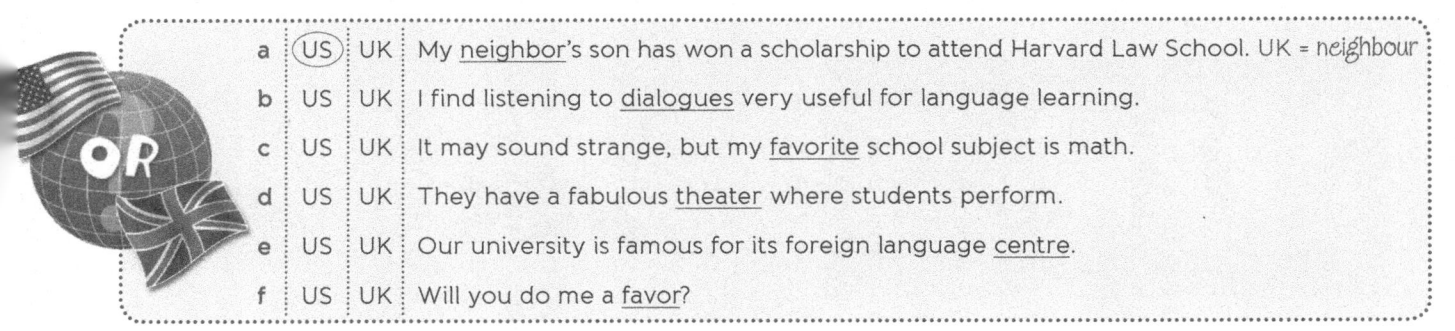

a (US) UK : My neighbor's son has won a scholarship to attend Harvard Law School. UK = neighbour
b US UK : I find listening to dialogues very useful for language learning.
c US UK : It may sound strange, but my favorite school subject is math.
d US UK : They have a fabulous theater where students perform.
e US UK : Our university is famous for its foreign language centre.
f US UK : Will you do me a favor?

2 Put the pairs with the correct flag. Find a list of US / UK words online and add two more useful pairs.

an apartment / a flat
a film / a movie
a cinema / a movie theater
a college student / a university student
a shop / a store
the chemist's / the drugstore
gas / petrol
a car park / a parking lot

3 Rewrite a-f as if you were regretting your choice.

a 'I didn't think carefully about my options.'
I should've thought more carefully about my options.
b 'Truth is I didn't get into law school 'cause I didn't work hard enough.'
I should've…
c 'Choosing engineering instead of art was a big mistake.'
I should've…
d 'Everybody says I didn't get the job because I didn't dress appropriately for the interview.'
I should…
e 'My career just isn't taking off 'cause I didn't go to music school when I had the chance, I guess.'
I should've…
f 'I dropped out of uni 'cause I wanted to make money straight away. Now I'm stuck in this boring, badly paid job.'
I shouldn't…

4 ▶ 4.8 Listen and express regrets. Follow the model.

Model: It was a mistake to drop out.
You: I shouldn't have dropped out.

5 ▶ 4.9 Order the phrases, 1-5, to make three dialogues a-c. Listen to check.

a ☐ Really? What did you do?
☐ I was in 5th grade, I think, and I stuck the teacher's handbag to a table.
☐ I have no idea. I really don't know.
☐ Why did you do such a thing?
[1] I did something terrible at school once.

b ☐ I looked my mother in the eye and told her that I hated her with all my heart.
☐ Really? What did you say?
☐ Yep! I don't really know where that came from.
☐ I said something really mean once.
☐ What a terrible thing to say!

c ☐ So I hit it off with my hand, but it hit the wall and broke into a thousand pieces. And I realised it wasn't an insect. It was some kind of brooch.
☐ Oh no! What a silly thing to do!
☐ I did the most embarrassing thing a while ago.
☐ This teacher came up to me and there was this insect on her blouse.
☐ Really? What did you do?

6 ▶ 4.10 Listen to extracts a-c, choose the correct option and react after the beep.

a Really? What did you **say** / **do**?
b Why would you **say** / **do** such a thing?
c What a silly thing to **say** / **do**!

4.3

21

4.4 What would you have said if you'd been late today?

1 Brad doesn't manage his time well. Match actions a-f to the results.

a I left revision to the last minute.
b I forgot to set the alarm.
c I got to the bus stop late.
d I arrived at the last minute.
e I didn't understand what to do.
f I failed the test.

- [ ] I missed the bus.
- [ ] I didn't complete the exercises correctly.
- [ ] I got my worst mark in English ever.
- [ ] I stayed up the night before the test to study.
- [ ] I missed the teacher's instructions.
- [ ] I didn't wake up in time to have breakfast before school.

2 ▶ 4.11 Complete Brad's regrets with the verbs. Listen to check and repeat.

a If I'd started to revise earlier, I _____ stay up all night studying. (not have to)
b If I'd remembered to set my alarm, I _____ in time to have breakfast before school. (wake up)
c If I _____ to the bus stop on time, I wouldn't have missed the bus. (get)
d If I _____ on time, I wouldn't have missed the teacher's instructions. (arrive)
e If I hadn't missed the teacher's instructions, I _____ what to do. (understand)
f If I'd done the exercises correctly, I _____. (pass)
g If I'd passed the test, I _____ my worst mark in English ever. (not get)

3 ▶ 4.12 Cross out the word with the different vowel sound. Listen to check.

a book – could – ~~shoe~~
b blue – two – push
c shoe – could – should
d true – would – through
e moved – moon – put
f pull – school – pool
g cook – woman – new

4 Match the words in 3 to the sound pictures.

5 (MAKE IT **PERSONAL**) Match embarrassing moments a-d to the titles. There is one extra. Then write two third conditional sentences for each.

- [ ] S... for stupid mobile phone
- [ ] Green isn't always good
- [ ] Man's worst friend
- [ ] The blue mobile phone
- [ ] 'Break' dance

a I took my dog for a walk before school. I stepped on the dog's mess. Back in class, my classmates traced the smell to my shoes and made fun of me.
If you hadn't taken _____

b I dropped my mobile phone. The girl I liked picked it up. She saw her face was the background on my phone and was really angry.

c I was dancing with a boy I liked. I did some crazy moves. I accidentally broke his nose.

d I was eating a hamburger with a girl I liked. A piece of lettuce leaf got stuck between my front teeth. The girl laughed in my face.

Cyber Tool

Think of an embarrassing moment (yours or a friend's). Write a three-sentence story, then summarise it with two third conditional sentences as in 5. Record it all and email it to a classmate.

Would you like to be a genius?

1 ▶4.13 Read film reviews 1-3 and complete them with **a**, **an** or **the**. Listen to check.

Film list #4: Geniuses

1 Vincent & Theo
Robert Altman directs __ fascinating film about what you need to be __ artist. Mainly, money. Tim Roth stars as famous impressionist artist Vincent van Gogh, who spends __ hours when he's not creating masterpieces trying to get money to create masterpieces. Paul Rhys plays his brother Theo, __ art gallery manager who tries to sell Vincent's work. __ film explores their complex relationship.

2 Little Man Tate
Jodie Foster's directorial debut is __ story of Fred (Adam Hann-Byrd), __ child prodigy. He can solve complicated maths problems and play piano incredibly well. Herself __ prodigy (as __ child actress), Foster–who also plays Fred's mother Dede–cleverly shows __ conflict between wanting to develop one's amazing gifts and needing to be __ normal child just like everyone else.

3 The Royal Tenenbaums
Director Wes Anderson's *Tenenbaums* is about __ family of three child geniuses–Margot (Gwyneth Paltrow), __ prodigy writer, Chas (Ben Stiller), __ young businessman, and Richie (Luke Wilson), __ pre-adolescent tennis star. Left by their father Royal (Gene Hackman) just as they began to do well in each of their respective fields, __ trio are now frustrated adults. Full of irony, exaggerated eccentricities, and __ talented cast, *Tenenbaums* is both funny and emotional.

2 Re-read and answer a-f.
- a How many actors are mentioned in the three reviews?
- b In these reviews, who is different from the others and why? Jodie Foster / Robert Altman / Wes Anderson / Ben Stiller.
- c Which film(s) is / are about child geniuses?
- d Which of the people mentioned in the reviews both direct and act in the same film?
- e Which film(s) is / are humorous?
- f Which of the film directors was a child prodigy?

3 Order the words in a-g and write sympathy (S) or criticism (C).
- a done / is / what's / done / .
- b thinking / were / what / you / ?
- c end / world / the / not / it's / the / of / .
- d better / you / known / should've / .
- e such / could / do / how / you / thing / a / ?
- f you / get / let / don't / it / down / .
- g you / will / learn / ever / ?

♪It's the end of the world as we know it, and I feel fine.♪ **4.5**

4 ▶4.14 Listen to problems 1-7 and react using expressions from 3. Follow the model.

'I didn't get the scholarship because I didn't prepare for the interview.'
Model: g
You: Will you ever learn?

5 ▶4.15 Complete the two sentences for each problem a-e. Listen to check.

a I didn't get the scholarship because I didn't prepare for the interview.
You (**should**/ shouldn't) 've prepared for the interview.
If you ('**d**/ hadn't) prepared for the interview, you would've got the scholarship.

b I failed the test because I didn't revise.
You (should / shouldn't) _____
If you ('d / hadn't) _____.

c I got really bad marks because I was absent a lot this semester.
You (should / shouldn't) _____
If you ('d / hadn't) _____.

d I got kicked out of school because I cheated in the exam.
You (should / shouldn't) _____
If you ('d / hadn't) _____.

e My parents were upset because I couldn't get into law school.
You (should / shouldn't) _____
If you ('d / hadn't) _____.

6 Find the connection between the song line above and the language of this lesson. Do the same with the other four song lines in unit 4 of the Student's Book.

Can you remember...
- 8 school words? SB→p.36
- 14 school subjects? SB→p.36
- 2 expressions with *do*, 2 with *get*, 1 with *make* and 1 with *take*? SB→p.37
- how to use *too* and *enough* with adjectives? SB→p.38
- the difference between /eɪt/ and /ət/ for *-ate* endings? SB→p.39
- 2 different spelling rules for UK and US English? SB→p.40
- ⊕, ⊖ and ⊘ for *should have*? SB→p.40
- ⊕ and ⊖ for third conditional? SB→p.43
- which syllable is stressed in three, four or five-syllable words ending in *-y*? SB→p.44
- 4 phrases for sympathy and 4 for criticism? SB→p.45

5 5.1 Are you a shopaholic?

1 Read the advice poster and match six of the titles a–i to tips 1–6.

a Think about the time you spend.
b Take control of the situation.
c Know yourself.
d Write down how much you spend.
e Do your feelings affect your shopping habits?
f Know when to find professional help.
g What is a shopaholic?
h Find healthy alternatives.
i Avoid unnecessary temptations.

6 ways to break a shopping compulsion.

If you or someone close to you has a problem with compulsive shopping and spending, these tips can help.

1 Compulsive spenders often hide or lie about their ____ and accumulate huge credit card debts. They often buy items they'll never use or wear, and even find them later with the price ____ still on them.

2 If you love-love-love to shop, ask yourself: Why? Just for the pleasure of it? Nothing better to do? Do you prefer to spend rather than ____? Are you crazy about certain items, like shoes, clothing or electrical items? Answering yes to any of these questions doesn't necessarily mean you have a problem, but if your spending is getting out of control, it's important to find out why.

3 Do you buy stuff when you're depressed, stressed, angry or lonely? Do you freak out every time you check your credit card ____? By understanding the feelings involved, you can focus on different ways to deal with them.

4 If your spending habits are affecting your life, stop buying in monthly ____. Start spending only what you have and only buy what you can ____. Pay for everything only in cash, by cheque or debit card. Cut up all credit cards except the one you use only for emergencies, but don't carry that card with you!

5 When you feel the impulse to go on a shopping ____, look for cheap ____ online or go ____ shopping, do something else. Life is short! Aren't there other things you could be doing? Go for a walk or do some exercise. This can distract you from the impulse until it passes.

6 If none of this works, and your spending is really out of control, look for counselling or therapy. Or try attending ____ anonymous meetings. Good luck—you can do it!

2 Re-read and complete with ten of these words.

afford	bargains	instalments	looking
parcel	purchases	save	shopaholics
spree	statement	tags	window

Cyber Tool
Choose the three best tips from a–i in 1 and email them to a classmate.

3 Underline five zero conditionals in the text.

4 Find 15 (3↘, 6→, 6↓) clothes and accessories in the word puzzle.

E	S	U	N	G	L	A	S	S	E	S
B	H	U	V	C	H	H	F	A	A	H
J	O	Z	I	O	A	C	J	V	R	O
K	R	F	Q	T	T	T	M	B	R	E
T	T	B	S	C	W	A	P	J	I	S
S	S	C	A	R	F	J	E	A	N	S
A	X	H	P	G	F	K	O	C	G	U
N	E	B	I	K	I	N	I	K	S	W
D	T	I	A	R	O	S	W	E	E	T
A	S	Y	N	E	T	A	A	T	R	T
L	J	E	W	E	L	L	E	R	Y	O
S	A	D	T	R	O	U	S	E	R	S

5 Which items from 4 complete phrases a–c?

a I bought <u>a new pair of</u> _____ last week. (7 items)
b I really want to buy <u>some</u> new _____. (8 items)
c That's <u>a</u> nice _____. (7 items)

6 ⏵ 5.1 Listen to six short phrases and write down the question you hear.

Cyber Tool
Are you a shopaholic? Make lists of 1) the last time you bought the items in 4 and 2) how much / many of each item you own. Share them with a classmate.

7 Read the cartoon and circle the correct answer a–f.

a The lady **is / isn't** going to buy the camera from the shop.
b The shop assistant **is / isn't** pleased to help her.
c This **is / isn't** a reason why independent shops are disappearing.
d I **found / didn't find** this funny.
e I've **done something similar / never done anything like this** myself.
f If I were the assistant, I **would / wouldn't** give her the number.

Have you ever borrowed money from a relative?

5.2

1 Read and match website messages a-f to the URLs.

a Treat your shopping addiction. Click to read our privacy policy.

b Welcome to your personal finance planner. Learn about investing and ways to save money.

c Up-to-the-minute financial news and statistics. Sign in.

d Up to 40% off outdoor toys and games. Shop now.

e Your card payment has been accepted. Thank you for shopping at Goalmart.

f Pay off your debt in 10 steps and maintain your lifestyle.

☐ www.financeguru.net/money/investments
☐ www.moneynumbersyouneednow.net/marketnews/regions
☐ www.stoptheshop.org/membership/privacy
☐ www.dontletdebtgetinyourway.com/credit/debtmanagement
☐ www.goalmart.com/electricals/LGxpt3-TV/payment/credit
☐ www.goalmart.com/kids/sales

2 ▶5.2 Listen to Jia and Andreas and complete the loan application form.

FREEFORT
Financial Services Ltd.

ACCESS Quick Money – Personal Loan Application

APPLICANT
Name: Andreas
Surname: Argyros
Net salary: £ _____ (tick as appropriate)
Weekly ☐
Monthly ☐
Annually ☐
Amount applied for: £ _____
Amount recommended: £ _____
Interest rate: _____ %
First payment date: _____, 2015.

GUARANTOR
Name: Dimitrios
Surname: Argyros
Relation (check as appropriate):
Parent ☐   Sibling ☐   Employer ☐   Other ☐

3 ▶5.3 Listen to extracts a-f and circle the word(s) you hear.

a My bank manager _____ approved a £2,000 loan.
has just / just / is just

b I did, but they only approved two grand. _____ make 500 quid a week, you know.
I only / We only / Only

c Did your brother _____ your guarantor?
agree to be / agree with / agree to see

d I guess _____ standard rate for a three-year loan.
it's the / is the / it's a

e _____ on the terms. When's your first payment due?
It depends / Depends / Depending

f _____ be able to pay it off?
Will you / Would you / Should you

4 ▶5.4 Listen and repeat a-f twice. Try to join the words together.

Cyber Tool

Use www.mailvu.com and talk about your shopping habits in 30 seconds in natural, connected English. Email it to a classmate.

5 ▶5.5 Put the words in the columns. Listen to check.

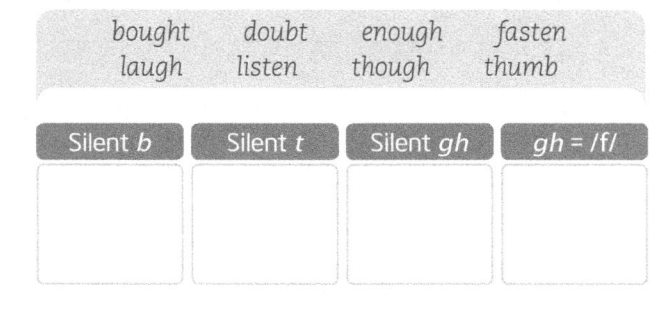

| bought | doubt | enough | fasten |
| laugh | listen | though | thumb |

Silent b	Silent t	Silent gh	gh = /f/

6 Complete signs and adverts a-e with the words from 5.

a Honest Pete's used cars. Cars _____ and sold.

b _____ your seat belt when the landing light is on.

c Place your _____ on the sensor for two seconds.

d College Comedy night. Look, _____ and _____ !

e 15 Cookies. 'We _____ that's _____ for you, _____ .'

5.3 Are you a good guesser?

1 Read the riddles a-e and complete guesses with the three words / expressions.

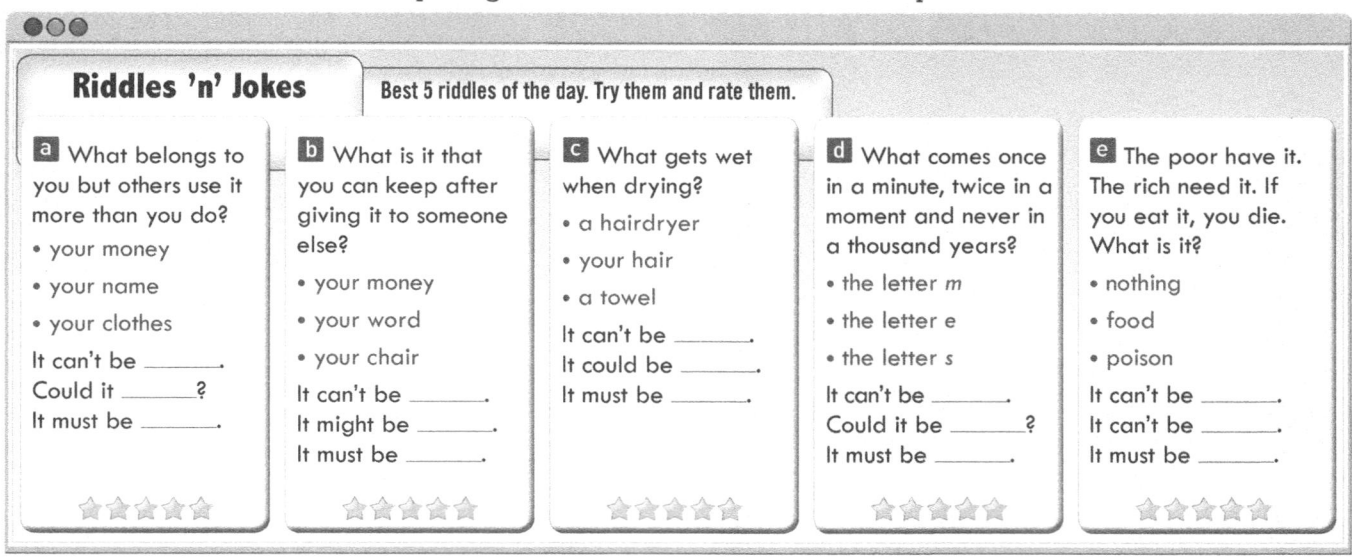

Riddles 'n' Jokes — Best 5 riddles of the day. Try them and rate them.

a What belongs to you but others use it more than you do?
- your money
- your name
- your clothes

It can't be _____.
Could it _____?
It must be _____.

b What is it that you can keep after giving it to someone else?
- your money
- your word
- your chair

It can't be _____.
It might be _____.
It must be _____.

c What gets wet when drying?
- a hairdryer
- your hair
- a towel

It can't be _____.
It could be _____.
It must be _____.

d What comes once in a minute, twice in a moment and never in a thousand years?
- the letter *m*
- the letter *e*
- the letter *s*

It can't be _____.
Could it be _____?
It must be _____.

e The poor have it. The rich need it. If you eat it, you die. What is it?
- nothing
- food
- poison

It can't be _____.
It can't be _____.
It must be _____.

2 ▶ 5.6 Listen and match 1-3 to three of the signs a-e.

a **American Airlines** Check-in Economy
b **MacArthur High School** Teacher's Meeting Room 3
c **MacArthur High School** Class of 2014
d **Gate 37** Now boarding
e **Live Show** Studio 4

3 Match statements a-f to the responses.

a There are figs on the menu.
b I've just run 20 km.
c Did you know that Lara doesn't drink milk?
d The boss asked to speak with me in her office.
e My credit card statement says I paid £60 for a pizza!
f Have you seen that new film? Absolutely terrible!

☐ Really? I guess she could be allergic or something.
☐ It could be a promotion. Good luck!
☐ That must mean that summer is nearly over.
☐ Come on! It got four stars. It can't be that bad.
☐ You must be exhausted. Come and sit down.
☐ What?! That can't be right.

4 Complete the mind maps with expressions from the box.

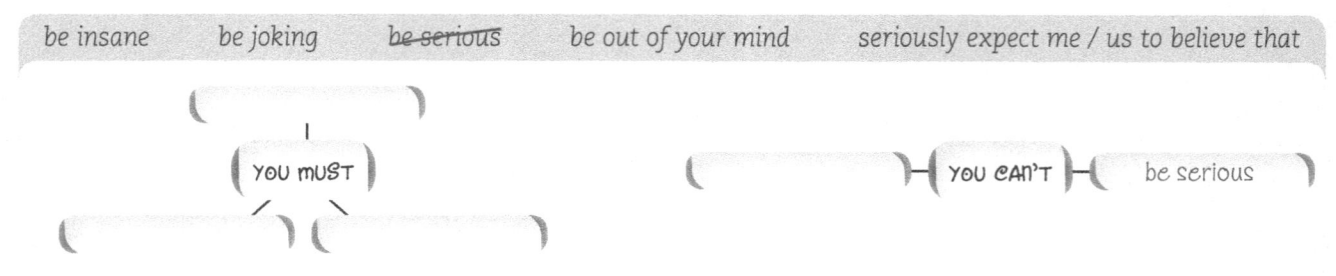

be insane   be joking   ~~be serious~~   be out of your mind   seriously expect me / us to believe that

(___)
(___) YOU MUST (___)
(___) (___)

(___) YOU CAN'T (be serious)

5 ▶ 5.7 Listen and tick the phrases from 4 you hear. Pay special attention to the way final **t** and **d** almost disappear before consonants.

6 ▶ 5.8 **Express surprise.** Listen and express surprise with the prompts. Follow the model.

Model: I just spent three thousand pounds on a designer bag. / be serious.
You: Three thousand pounds? You can't be serious!

Have you ever bought a useless product?

5.4

1 Quickly read and match photos a-d to the four sale items.

WEIRD STUFF

Into bargain-hunting online? Here are a few examples of the most bizarre things ever sold on eBay's auction site:

☐ The owner of an F/A-18 Hornet fighter jet had bought it second-hand and had offered to have the plane restored for an incredibly low price of $9,000,000. After hearing of the auction, the FBI immediately notified the seller that he could only sell the plane to an American citizen residing in the United States. On top of that, the plane could not leave US airspace; it was a matter of national security. Under these circumstances, nobody was prepared to participate in the auction.

☐ After Britney Spears had her hair cut off completely, the hairdresser's put it on eBay. The owner obviously saw the opportunity to make a small fortune. However, due to eBay's policy, the ambitious owner was not able to complete the transaction.

☐ One of the most interesting auctions happened in November 2005 when the original 1923 Hollywood sign was sold on eBay. The owner at the time wanted to sell it because he needed the money to finance a Hollywood project. A prospective buyer had a team of experts brought in to certify that it was indeed an original. Luckily it was, and the transaction was completed successfully.

☐ There are many unbelievable stories. A citizen of Australia tried to sell the country of New Zealand once. Ridiculous! There were a couple of bidders that day, but the auction suddenly stopped because it violated eBay's policy. I guess it's impossible to sell a country unless its people agree to it.

2 Re-read it. How many of the items were actually sold?

Cyber Tool
What weird item would you like to put on eBay? Your local bus? A politician? Record and email your ideas to a classmate.

I'd put all the pigeons from my city...

3 ▶ 5.9 Complete the suffix table with 12 words from the text. Circle the stress. Listen to check.

Nouns	Verbs	Adjectives	Adverbs
a(bi)lity	sol(u)tion	(pu)rify	(gor)geous	re(mar)kable	(des)perately

4 Complete a-f with the correct form of the words in brackets.
 a Dial 0800 3347171 to _____ your reservation now. (security)
 b I'd never used such a _____ product before. (marvel)
 c The thing turned out to be a complete _____. (disappoint)
 d The label said it was _____, but I guess I should've had it dry-cleaned. (wash)
 e I love to see all those shirts _____ arranged on the shelves. (nice)
 f The shop assistant said the cream would _____ my skin. (pure)

5 Are the adjectives in infomercials 1-5 in the correct order? Tick the correct ones and correct the incorrect ones.

Five more weird products!

1 Introducing the one and only Cat translator, a electronic revolutionary device that will allow you and your pet to communicate like you've never dreamed possible.

2 This is the ultra-absorbent amazing towel with arm openings that keeps you totally covered and allows you to move your arms freely.

3 Introducing the practical fully automatic egg cooker that cooks up to six eggs simultaneously to perfect consistency in minutes.

4 This is the air-conditioned innovative shirt that keeps you cool when you most need it.

5 Tired of not understanding people from other countries? Try the wireless fantastic earpiece that translates every language perfectly for you!

5.5 Do you often buy things on impulse?

♪ Shopping for labels, shopping for love. Manolo and Louis, it's all I'm thinking of. ♪

1 Read the four headings in the article and predict what the article is about, a-c. Then read enough to confirm your choice.

a How gender influences our attitude to shopping.
b Why men hate shopping.
c How men's and women's present attitudes to shopping link back to our evolutionary past.

▶ Why women shop while men wait outside

Many men and women agree that shopping together only causes stress. Why is it that women can spend hours trying on clothes, and men can't wait to get out just a short time after they get in?

▶ 'Man hunt buffalo, woman pick berries'

According to one scientist, Dr Kruger, it's the way we evolved. Historically the man's job was to provide meat: go out, find an animal, catch it quickly and quietly before it escapes. Women, on the other hand, had to bring home fruit and vegetables: find a tree, carefully select the best berries and bring home lots of them.

▶ Picking fruit is social, hunting is solitary

Kruger believes that the different methods of finding food meant that men and women developed different practical skills. Men learned to find their way easily, which allowed them to identify 'dinner', kill it and return home by the shortest route. Sort of like the way a guy picks out an anniversary card. Women, however, went by instinct or previous experience and probably found food with other females. It was a social event, like today's shopping sprees.

▶ Understanding gender differences

Although men don't really have a 'kill' instinct when shopping for trousers, Kruger still insists his data strongly shows that modern women use ancient skills while shopping. Kruger hopes his ideas will help to take the stress out of shopping and it seems that's already happening in parts of Europe. In Germany they have places where men can kill time, have a few beers and play with electronic devices while their partner goes shopping!

23

2 Re-read 1 carefully and circle the correct choices in a-f.

a Men **like / don't like** to spend a lot of time at the shops.
b Early man had to be **quick and quiet / slow and careful** to kill animals for food.
c The way women shop is **similar to / different from** the way they used to pick fruit.
d **Being close to home / Not getting lost** was important for hunters.
e Modern men **feel / don't feel** like killing when they go shopping.
f German retailers **seem to / don't seem to** understand how gender influences shopping habits.

3 ▶ 5.10 Order sentences a-f. Write customer (C) or shop assistant (SA). Listen to check.

☐ I just need to see your receipt, please.
☐ Can I exchange it for the 256 GB?
☐ I bought this flash drive yesterday and realised it's only 63 GB instead of the 256 GB I paid for.
☐ In that case I'm afraid there's nothing I can do.
☐ Seriously? But look, I have the bag.
☐ That's the thing. I threw it away, you see.

4 ▶ 5.11 Complete the dialogue with five words from the box. Listen to check.

card   cash   declined   dial   enter
last   password   pin   thanks

SA	_____ or charge?
C	Charge, please.
SA	Thank you. _____ your pin, please.
C	There you go.
SA	I'm afraid your card has been _____.
C	I don't understand. Can you try this one?
SA	Sure. _____, please.
C	Here we go again.
SA	It worked this time. There you are.
C	Ah! At _____!

5 ▶ 5.12 **Dictation.** Listen and write down a dialogue. Check your answer in the AS on p. 55.

6 Find the connection between the song line above and the language of this lesson. Do the same with the other four song lines in unit 5 of the Student's Book.

Can you remember...

▸ the name for a compulsive chocolate eater? SB→p. 48
▸ 5 prepositional phrases with *in* and 2 with *on*? SB→p. 49
▸ how to use *borrow* and *lend*? SB→p. 50
▸ how much a grand + 100 quid + 3 fivers + a tenner is? SB→p. 51
▸ 4 things you can run out of? SB→p. 52
▸ 5 modals of probability? SB→p. 53
▸ 3 portmanteau words? SB→p. 54
▸ 2 examples of words with the suffixes -*ous*, -*ment* and -*ness*? SB→p. 55
▸ adjective order? SB→p. 55

Are you addicted to TV?

1 Read the text and order the article title.

Makes / What / Addictive / Ever / Than / Today's / Before / Series / More / ?

☐ Sitting down in front of the TV to watch your favourite programme is becoming a thing of the past. Binge watching, which means watching several episodes one after another, is growing and it seems to be how more and more of us want our TV. The best programme creators are beginning to understand that too.

☐ According to him, the majority of 20th-century programmes, including great dramas like *The Sopranos* and *Six Feet Under*, had episodes that worked independently. If you missed one, it didn't matter too much. In the early 2000s, programmes like *24*, a series by Fox, started to change that. Viewers really needed to watch every episode to understand the story and soon, the 12- or 13-episode serialised drama had become a new American art form.

☐ The adult themes, antiheroes and the art direction make them look like films. But, while older programmes focused on the characters, today's also focus on what happens next. Series creators are beginning to create stories that are less obvious. Series like *Lost*, for example, tell stories with more unexpected occurrences and a lot more suspense.

☐ After watching our favourite series, we feel relaxed, our brains rest and our bodies fill with endorphins, our natural 'feel-good substance'. Maybe that's why we feel happy as soon as we switch the TV on and then watch several episodes at once to satisfy our 'addiction'.

☐ Before DVDs and Internet streaming, TV viewers had two choices: (1) watch whatever happened to be on, no matter how idiotic; or (2) turn the TV off and feel frustrated. Now we have a third: watch the programmes we like, whenever we like and for as long as we like. Serialised, streaming TV is perfect for keeping the endorphins flowing, and TV writers know it.

2 Choose the correct alternative in a-e and match the sentences to the paragraphs.

a TV producers **have / having** discovered this science, and by **use / using** new technology, they have given TV fans a third option.

b Apparently, **have / having** to watch more before you can understand what's going on makes modern series more and more addictive.

c How we watch TV **has / have** been changing in recent years.

d New series like *The Walking Dead* **is / are** similar to serials from the past in some ways.

e D B Weiss, a writer for *Game of Thrones*, **told / said** *Newsweek* how he thinks things are changing.

3 Complete a-e with prepositions. Then re-read the article. True (T) or false (F)?

a According _____ the article, some programme creators have detected changes in traditional TV viewing patterns.

b Fox was very influential in changing TV programmes at the end _____ the last century.

c Modern series usually have more complex storylines _____ series from the past.

d If you have to watch _____ a long time to understand a story, you get tired and stop watching.

e Today's viewers don't need to feel frustrated if there's nothing of interest _____ TV.

4 ▶ 6.1 Match both columns to form media words. Listen to check and mark the stress.

a live ☐ drama
b medical ☐ media
c the ☐ operas
d reality ☐ news
e soap ☐ show
f social ☐ sites
g chat ☐ sport
h web ☐ TV

5 Study the first column in 4 and find:
- 3 nouns
- 3 adjectives
- 1 verb
- 1 article

6 ▶ 6.2 Listen to five dialogues and match items a-h in 4 to the speakers. There's one extra item.

1 The man's addicted to ☐.
  The woman prefers ☐.
2 This lady just loves ☐.
  This guy is addicted to ☐.
3 Both of them really like ☐.
4 They are both addicted to ☐.
5 They're always watching ☐.

Cyber Tool

Record your TV preferences. What do you like to watch? When do you like to watch it? Share your video with a classmate. Any differences?

6.2 What's your favourite TV programme?

1 Complete a-f with *a*, *an*, *the* or prepositions. Read the article. True (T) or false (F)?

a ___ programmes are ___ order ___ popularity.
b ___ US has made more seasons of ___ Survivor than the UK.
c ___ man ___ The Bachelor always proposes.
d The Osbournes was successful largely because ___ Ozzy's popularity.
e Viewers only want to see ___ good singers ___ X Factor.
f All ___ ___ celebrities ___ Strictly Come Dancing are extremely famous.

The Five Reality TV Shows that Had the Biggest Impact this Century

Twenty years ago, with the exception of the news and documentaries, the people on TV were all actors who had learned from scripts. There weren't many 'real' people, but everything changed in 1997 with a show called *Survivor*. Now it seems reality TV is here to stay. Here are some of our favourites, in no particular order.

Survivor
Since starting in Sweden in 1997, 48 different countries and regions have used the programme's format. A cast of strangers are sent to an island or jungle location and have to live without modern luxuries until the final winner gets a prize. The British version only ran for two seasons although there have been 28 seasons in the US!

The Bachelor
This show focuses on a group of women who live together and compete for a handsome guy's marriage proposal. There have been four proposals in the British version since the show started in 2003.

The Osbournes
If you were a star, would you open your home to TV cameras 24/7? Ozzy Osbourne and his wife Sharon Osbourne did exactly that. *The Osbournes* attracted millions of viewers, who loved it because they realised that celebrities were a mess just like regular people.

X Factor
The *X Factor* debuted in 2004, the creation of *Pop Idol* (and *American Idol*) judge Simon Cowell. *X Factor* is more than just a talent show, it's a sensation! Many feel *X Factor*'s attraction is the auditions. They are open to all and we see the best singers and the very worst!

Strictly Come Dancing
Who wants to see a celebrity dance salsa? Apparently, millions of us do. This show became an instant hit in 2004. Part of the success comes from showing a vulnerable side of celebrities, some minor and some big names, as they struggle to learn a new skill.

2 Correct the mistakes in a-d and match them to the programmes in 1.

a The contestant who she is leaving the island this week is Fifi.
b The women who lives in the house want to get married.
c The island what we chose is very beautiful.
d Kelly Osbourne recorded 'Papa Don't Preach', a song that it was originally performed by Madonna.

3 Combine the two sentences in a-g with *that*, *who* or *whose*.

a Nicki Minaj and Mariah Carey are judges. Their fights on camera were popular on Twitter.
b Catherine is the girl. She won the diamond engagement ring.
c The location is usually far away from civilisation. The organisers choose it.
d Ozzy is a famous heavy metal vocalist. His family appeared on MTV.
e Kim's the woman. She won after the other 14 contestants left the island.
f He's chosen a song. The song is close to his heart.
g The dances can be difficult. The professionals teach them the dances.

4 ▶ 6.3 Cross out four relative pronouns that are not necessary. Listen to check and repeat.

HELP US IMPROVE YOUR TV
Please take a moment to do our questionnaire.
1 How often is the team that you support on TV?
2 Are there any TV presenters who you can't stand? Who?
3 Would you like to see more programmes that have 'real' people?
4 Do you prefer films that make you laugh or cry?
5 Are there any theme songs that you like to sing? Which one(s)?
6 Do you like news anchors who make jokes?
7 Are there any programmes that you'd like to prohibit? Which one(s)?

Cyber Tool

Record your answers in 4 and share with a classmate. Any surprises?

5 ▶ 6.4 Complete forum replies a-d with a *turn* expression. Listen to check.

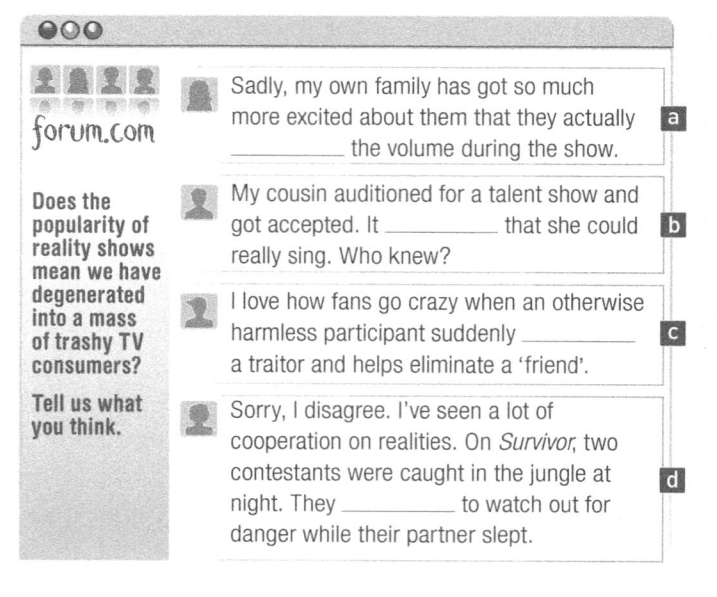

Does the popularity of reality shows mean we have degenerated into a mass of trashy TV consumers? Tell us what you think.

a Sadly, my own family has got so much more excited about them that they actually ___ the volume during the show.
b My cousin auditioned for a talent show and got accepted. It ___ that she could really sing. Who knew?
c I love how fans go crazy when an otherwise harmless participant suddenly ___ a traitor and helps eliminate a 'friend'.
d Sorry, I disagree. I've seen a lot of cooperation on realities. On *Survivor*, two contestants were caught in the jungle at night. They ___ to watch out for danger while their partner slept.

What were the last three films you saw? 6.3

1 Read and match a–f to the sentence endings. There is one extra.

a Adele's song 'Skyfall' has made Bond films…
b The James Bond franchise…
c *Star Wars* is popular…
d The films have made billions for Fox…
e *Harry Potter* is popular with…
f The Harry Potter franchise…

☐ and Lucasfilm over more than three decades.
☐ attractive for a younger generation of moviegoers.
☐ will probably have many more films in future.
☐ is over 50 years old.
☐ was filmed in the UK.
☐ all over the world.
☐ young and old movie fans.

2 ▶ 6.5 Read the text and complete the **bold** phrases with *that*, *which*, *who* or *whose*. Insert commas where necessary. Listen to check.

Top 3 movie franchises ever

Hollywood franchises. A good one will make billions of dollars in ticket sales and brand-related merchandise for many decades.

Nº1 — JAMES BOND. 24 MOVIES. $14 BILLION +

Since 1962, this seemingly endless franchise has been introducing moviegoers to a glamorous spy world. **Daniel Craig ___ is the latest Mr Bond** and superstar **Adele ___ single 'Skyfall' played all over the world for months** were both cleverly chosen to attract a younger audience. The next generation of Bond addicts has been secured.

Nº2 — STAR WARS. 6 MOVIES. $9 BILLION +

The franchise ___ has reached every corner of the planet. Six movies, or seven if you count *Clone Wars*, and more than three decades of comics, TV series, radio programmes, toys, games, Blu-ray and branded merchandise have been very profitable for both for Fox and **George Lucas ___ created and directed most of the movies**. May the force be with you, George.

Nº3 — HARRY POTTER. 8 MOVIES. $8 BILLION +

The magical franchise for both kids and adults was inspired by author **J K Rowling ___ novels sold millions of copies to all age groups**. The books ___ were mainly written in a café have made her millions. It may take a few years, but it seems inevitable that there will one day be more battles involving the witches and **wizards ___ she created**.

3 Find three relative clauses in each film description and mark them restrictive (R) or non-restrictive (N).

Films in three sentences!

Spider-Man, who was originally a Marvel superhero, has had five films. The fourth one premiered in 2012 with a cast that included a new Spider-Man played by Andrew Garfield. Mary Jane Parker, who was the love interest between 2002 and 2007, was cut from the 2012 and 2014 films.

Author Stephanie Meyer, whose novels inspired five films so far, must be pretty pleased with the amazing success of her *Twilight* saga. These vampire films, which have captivated teenagers worldwide, tell of beautiful hair, perfect bodies, dreamy kisses and the violent battles that the Cullens and their wolf friends fight against the Volturi. It's exciting stuff!

4 ▶ 6.6 Insert two speech pauses (/) in four of sentences a–e. Listen to check and repeat with pauses and intonation. Which sentence doesn't have speech pauses? Why?

a *The Dark Knight* which is my favourite Batman movie won four Oscars.
b Heath Ledger who played the scariest Joker ever seen won an Academy Award after he died.
c Christian Bale who played Batman wasn't nominated for an Oscar for his part.
d Johnny Depp is the actor that has made Jack Sparrow so unforgettable.
e *Pirates of the Caribbean* which was inspired by Disneyworld's attraction has made over 5 billion dollars so far.

6.4 Where do you usually watch films?

1 Match the columns to make quotes a-e. Complete with **as** or **like**. Which one do you like best?

a Fame is _____ caviar, you know?
b Wealth is _____ seawater; the more we drink,
c I just use my muscles
d Fame, you know, it's _____ a hand gun—
e Don't quit! Suffer now

☐ and live the rest of your life _____ a champion. Muhammad Ali (boxer)
☐ It's good to have it, but not when you have it at every meal. Marilyn Monroe (actress)
☐ in the wrong hands, it's dangerous. Matthew Morrison (actor)
☐ the thirstier we become; and the same is true of fame. Arthur Schopenhauer (philosopher)
☐ _____ a conversation starter. Arnold Schwarzenegger (actor)

2 ▶6.7 Listen to this joke warning and answer a-g.

a What's the name of the virus?
b Is it safe to touch?
c What can it destroy?
d What's the antidote?
e What are three places it can be found?
f Who should you send the message to?
g And if you can't do that, what does it mean?

3 ▶6.8 Order words in a-e to make more advice for sufferers. Listen to check and repeat.

a on / you / go / time / sure / make / home / .
b about / a / think / holiday / having / .
c enough / to / always / water / have / drink / .
d do / try / you / more / can / to / never / than / .
e take / more / you / efficient / you'll / if / breaks, / be / regular / .

4 ▶6.9 Look at the celebrities and do the quiz. Listen for more clues and match 1-6 to the photos.

Celebrity Guess Who...?

How many stars can you recognise? Who did what before getting lucky?

1 Which pop singer started her career as a **country / church** singer?
2 Which artist won a Barbadian **beauty / swimming** competition as a teenager?
3 Which singer earned her living as a **car park / McDonald's** attendant?
4 Which film star worked as a **taxi driver / hotel porter** before becoming a star?
5 Who worked as a **tobacco cutter / dancer** in Kentucky before moving to LA?
6 Which star has credits as a **songwriter / singer** for The Pussycat Dolls and Jennifer Lopez?

Cyber Tool
Record yourself talking about jobs that you / your parents have / had in the past. Share with a classmate.

5 Circle the verbs used with **as** in 4.

When was the last time you did something crazy?

♪ Makes me feel like I can't live without you. ♪

6.5

1 Complete the quiz with *in* or *on*.

In and On Quiz!

Who are the three people that have had the most influence _____ you?
What are three things you have _____ a wall _____ your house?
What are three things you only wear _____ winter?
What is the worst programme currently _____ TV?
What is the last thing you paid for _____ instalments?
What are three important dates _____ history?
What is the last video you watched _____ YouTube?
When was the last time you went shopping _____ your own?

Cyber Tool

Choose two **in** and two **on** questions. Record your answers and share with a classmate. Did you choose the same things? Any surprises?

2 Complete a–e with prepositions then read the article. True (T) or false (F)?

a All celebrities are famous _____ their talents.
b If you don't look the same _____ others, people might think you're a celebrity.
c After some time, you could wear clothes made _____ meat or vegetables.
d Your friends' sense of fashion isn't as important _____ your own.
e If your father looks _____ a chauffeur, everybody will think you are a star.

CHEAT'S GUIDE TO LIVING LIKE A STAR

We see them on TV and read about them in magazines. Today there is no escape from the celebrity lifestyle and there is a growing number of celebrities who are famous for... er, well... being famous. But why go to the trouble of learning to sing, auditioning for a film or embarrassing yourself on a reality TV show? Follow our tips and you could live the life of a celebrity, kind of.

1. Get noticed. This really is the most important part. If you look different and stand out from the crowd, people will want to know what your secret is (whatever you tell them, don't tell the truth!). Now, of course, we don't recommend that you instantly follow Lady Gaga's example and go out wearing clothes made of meat (especially if you live in a neighbourhood with a lot of dogs). Start small and work up to meat dresses (or vegetables if you're a vegetarian). Try a new hairstyle and maybe some accessories.

2. Accessories. Think of accessories as more than just clothes. Accessorising is a lifestyle! From the phone you use to the friends you hang out with—everything has to make YOU look good. OK... it might be that your current friends don't have the 'right' sense of fashion and style to show you at your best. It's time to get serious. Drop those friends and find new ones that match your new glamorous lifestyle a little better. And if you can't find any new friends, get a dog.

3. Followers. Every celebrity needs followers. You know, those people who go around with them hoping to become famous as well. Of course, there are the professional followers too—think security guards, drivers, photographers. You won't be able to afford all of these people just yet, but that shouldn't be a problem. Try asking your dad to wear a suit and sunglasses when he drives you to the nearest nightclub; everybody will think he is your personal driver.

3 ▶ 6.10 Listen and tick the best summary.

The girls are talking about:
a what stars demand in their dressing rooms.
b what female stars expect in their dressing rooms.

4 ▶ 6.10 Listen again and circle the correct answers in a–f. Check in the AS on p. 56.

a They say Beyoncé requires **baked** / **fried** chicken.
b Katy Perry insists her room be **painted** / **furnished** in a **specific** / **colourful** way.
c Lynn can't believe that Katy wants a **series** / **pair** of **French lamps** / **lights**.
d Britney often requested a photo **of** / **that belonged to** Lady Diana.
e Rihanna has a **long** / **short** list of things she likes to **eat** / **drink**.
f If you get in free to **a Rihanna** / **an Adele** show, **you must** / **she will** give money to charity.

5 ▶ 6.11 Follow the model.

Model: I heard Adele wants cigarettes in her dressing room. / No way!
You: She wants cigarettes? No way!

6 Find the connection between the song line above and the language of this lesson. Do the same with the other four song lines in unit 6 of the Student's Book.

Can you remember...

- 12 TV genres? SB → p. 60
- 2 ways of watching foreign films? SB → p. 60
- what *stream* and *trend* mean? SB → p. 61
- 4 expressions with *turn*? SB → p. 62
- how to use restrictive & non-restrictive relative clauses? SB → p. 126
- the difference between *as* and *like* in comparisons? SB → p. 66
- 8 items that use *on* and 5 that use *in*? SB → p. 68
- 5 expressions to show surprise? SB → p. 69

7

7.1 Does technology drive you mad?

1 Cross out ten car parts in the word snake to find two car producers. Which one do you prefer?

> meclutchrcebrakedebonnetsbeenginensteeringwheelzvacceleratorobootlktyreswwiperswagwindscreenen

2 ▶ 7.1 Listen to five parts of a conversation. Match the 'beeps' to car parts in the snake in 1.
Part 1 _____, 2 _____, 3 _____, 4 _____, 5 _____.

3 ▶ 7.2 Complete a–d with car parts from 1. Listen to check.
a When driving, you must use your right foot both for the _____ and the _____.
b That _____ is so dirty! How can you see the road?
c I'm sorry I'm late. I had to stop to change a flat _____.
d My new car has a 2.0 litre _____. It's much faster than my old one!

4 Complete with **on**, **off**, **up** or **down**. Match a–f to the photos.
a My feet are killing me! Can you take _____ my shoes for me, please?
b This is driving me mad! Would you mind turning _____ the music a bit?
c You're wasting too much electricity. Why don't you switch _____ some of those lights?
d It's kind of cold outside. Here, put _____ this coat.
e Could you turn _____ the heat, please? It's not warm enough in here.
f Could you turn _____ the lights, please? It's too dark in here!

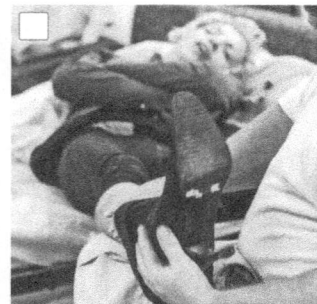

5 Reply to the requests in 4. Use a pronoun and say 'yes' to them all.
a OK, I'll take them off.
b OK, I'll turn _____.
c OK, I'll _____.
d OK, _____.
e _____
f _____

6 ▶ 7.3 Replace the object with a pronoun. Follow the model.

Model: *Please turn up the volume.*
You: *Please turn it up.*
Model: *Let's switch on the lights.*
You: *Let's switch them on.*

What was the last little lie you told?

7.2

1 Read and complete the blog entry with **say** or **tell**.

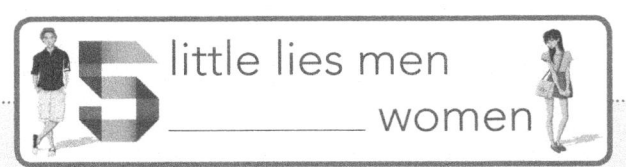

5 little lies men _____ women

There are many lies we men _____ women in a relationship. These lies are not intended to hurt or deceive our partners, but to prevent potential problems from happening.
These are five of the most common little lies.

1 'You don't look fat.'
Just before you go out for a fun night, you might hear 'Do I look fat in this?' The only possible answer to this question is to _____ 'No, you don't', even if the truth is 'Maybe just a little'. And never, ever, _____ 'It doesn't matter, baby. I like you just the way you are!' She'll hate you forever for that!

2 'You are a great cook.'
This is a dangerous lie to _____ your woman, because if you're planning to live a large part of your life with her, you'll have to _____ the truth at some point!

3 'I don't look at other women.'
This little lie helps a woman's confidence. She'll know you're lying, because all women know that all men like to look at other women. But most women will be OK with that lie—if you don't _____ it too often!

4 'I like romantic comedies.'
Very often we'll _____ that and sit through the film, just because it won't hurt to please her. Like most of the lies men tell women, this one is designed to make everybody's life easier.

5 'I'm sorry.'
When you _____ that, you can stop many little disagreements becoming major fights, even if you don't really mean it. This is one of the first little lies you ever told and one of the most used.

What is really essential is to know that as long as you use lies in moderation, it shouldn't cause problems in a healthy relationship.

Read next week's post for five lies that women tell men!

2 Re-read and answer a-e. Which lie 1-5…

a is risky because in the end you will have to tell the truth? _____
b is the most common? _____
c is safe to tell, although women will know it isn't the truth? _____
d must be told at all costs? _____
e is often told just to make women happy? _____

3 ▶ 7.4 Diana's ex told her the five lies from 1. Change the underlined pronouns and verbs in lies 1-5, and complete her complaints. Listen to check.

He's a liar!

1 He said _____!
And I'd just burned our dinner!

2 He said _____.
But I could see myself in the mirror. I was huge!

3 He said _____,
and then he fell asleep when we watched one!

4 He said _____,
but he could never keep his eyes off my friends!

5 He said _____,
but I knew he didn't mean it at all!

4 ▶ 7.5 Listen and report lies a-f with the correct pronouns (P) and verbs (V).

a He said the cheque (V)_____ in the mail.
b He said (P)_____ (V)_____ pay next time.
c She said (P)_____ (V)_____ still be good friends.
d He told Carol (P)_____ (V)_____ great.
e She told Tina (P)_____ (V)_____ him for his money.
f He said it (V)_____ never happened to (P)_____ before.

5 Use **told** to report Anna and Mark's dialogue, if possible. If not, use **said**. Change pronouns and verbs as necessary. Follow the example.

'I'll marry you, Anna!'
'I've never been interested in marriage.'
'I know you love me, Anna!'
'I can't marry you, Mark! I'm in love with someone else.'

Mark told Anna he would marry her.

Cyber Tool

What's your worst lie ever? Record your answer and share it with a classmate.

I once told a friend / my mother that…

7.3 Are you confident with technology?

1 ▶ 7.6 Listen to Mr Keller's call. Who's he getting help from?

a A help desk agent.
b A friend who's good with computers.
c His wife of 20 years.

2 ▶ 7.6 Which five questions of a–g did you hear? Listen again to check.

a What kind of tablet do you have? ☐
b Have you installed iTunes on your computer? ☐
c What are you talking about? ☐
d Are you familiar with the different icons? ☐
e Do you have a Mac or a PC? ☐
f When did you buy it? ☐
g How can I upload music to my tablet? ☐

3 ▶ 7.7 These indirect question phrases are in phonetics. Can you decipher them? Listen to check and repeat.

a /kən jʊ tel miː/
b /aɪ wʌndə(r) ɪf/
c /aɪ hæv nʊ aɪdɪə ɪf/
d /aɪ niːd tə nəʊ ɪf/
e /də jʊ nəʊ ɪf/
f /də jʊ hæv eniː aɪdɪə/
g /kəd jʊ tel miː/

4 Change a–g in 2 to indirect questions. Use the phrases from 3.

a Can you tell me what kind of tablet you have?
b I wonder if _____
c _____
d _____
e _____
f _____
g _____

5 ▶ 7.8 Listen to the random question generator and change the questions into indirect questions.

RANDOM QUESTION GENERATOR

THEY WANT TO KNOW...
A how old I am.
B _____
C _____
D _____
E _____
F _____

⏻ Cyber Tool

Record 1) your answers to a–f and 2) what you would ask your country's president if you met him / her face to face. Send them to a classmate.

I'd ask him / her if / where / what / when / why / how…

6 ▶ 7.9 Write the words with **bold** letters in the correct sound column. Listen and repeat a–e to check.

a Never p**u**ll the pl**u**g out by the power cable.
b Please p**u**sh the green b**u**tton to c**u**t off the power.
c P**u**t this c**u**shion **u**nder you to get more c**o**mfortable.
d If you can't sh**u**t the browser window, it might be a b**u**g.
e Don't let your noteb**oo**k inbox get too f**u**ll.

ʊ	ʌ

Are machines with personality a good idea?

7.4

1 Thais is telling her sister about the questions in her oral test yesterday. Read what she said and complete the original questions.

a First they asked how old I was.   'How old ___are you___?'
b They asked what I did last weekend.   '_____ last weekend?'
c They asked if I liked studying.   '_____ studying?'
d They asked when I would finish school.   'When _____ school?'
e They asked if I was going to have a party.   '_____ going to have a party?'
f They asked how much my English had improved.   'How much _____ English _____?'

2 Correct the mistake in sentences a-e.

a Sue asked me to not ring her tonight.
b I asked her where was she going.
c She asked me why did I want to know.
d I told her to not be rude to me.
e She said me to leave her alone.

3 A traveller is going through customs with a new phone. Are a-h requests (R) or real questions (Q)?

a Did you buy that phone in this country, madam?
b Can you let me see it, please?
c Do I have to pay duty on it?
d How am I supposed to do that?
e Could you hold on while I ask my supervisor?
f Which carrier are you using?
g Can you get a signal here?
h Would you fill out this form, please?

4 ▶ 7.10 Match a-h to the gaps in the blog. Listen to Andy talking to a friend to check.

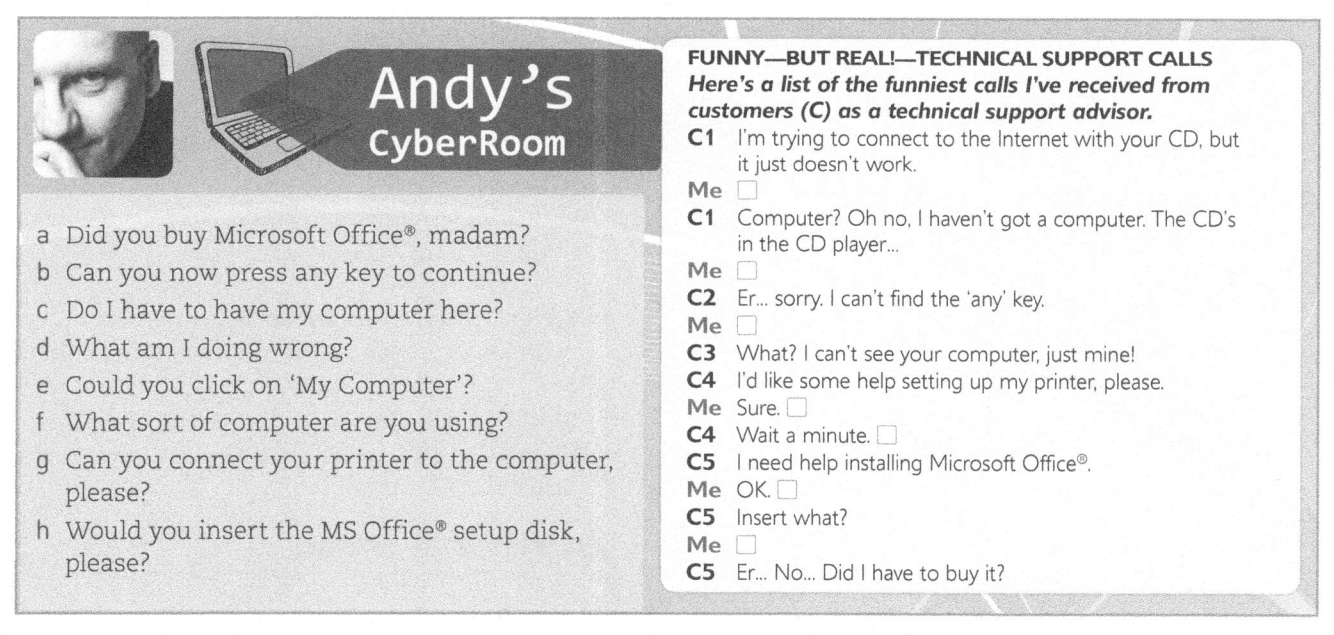

Andy's CyberRoom

a Did you buy Microsoft Office®, madam?
b Can you now press any key to continue?
c Do I have to have my computer here?
d What am I doing wrong?
e Could you click on 'My Computer'?
f What sort of computer are you using?
g Can you connect your printer to the computer, please?
h Would you insert the MS Office® setup disk, please?

FUNNY—BUT REAL!—TECHNICAL SUPPORT CALLS
Here's a list of the funniest calls I've received from customers (C) as a technical support advisor.

C1 I'm trying to connect to the Internet with your CD, but it just doesn't work.
Me ☐
C1 Computer? Oh no, I haven't got a computer. The CD's in the CD player...
Me ☐
C2 Er... sorry. I can't find the 'any' key.
Me ☐
C3 What? I can't see your computer, just mine!
C4 I'd like some help setting up my printer, please.
Me Sure. ☐
C4 Wait a minute. ☐
C5 I need help installing Microsoft Office®.
Me OK. ☐
C5 Insert what?
Me ☐
C5 Er... No... Did I have to buy it?

5 Re-read. True (T) or false (F)?

a C1 can't connect to the Internet because he hasn't got a CD.
b C2 thinks 'any key' is a specific key on the keyboard.
c C3 doesn't understand what 'My Computer' is.
d C4 can't set up his printer because he hasn't got his computer.
e C5 can't install MS Office® because her disk is not working.

6 ▶ 7.11 Report the requests or commands to help an old lady at the doctor's. Tell her what the doctor said. Follow the model.

Doctor: Sit down.
You: He asked you to sit down.
Doctor: Could you please open your mouth?
You: He asked you to open your mouth.

7.5 Do you spend too much time on social networks?

♪ We found love in a hopeless place ♪

1 Match the activities a-f.

a social
b visiting
c studying for
d leisure
e playing
f watching

☐ reading
☐ online films
☐ video games
☐ museums
☐ networking
☐ tests

2 (MAKE IT PERSONAL) Make a-d true using activities from 1.

a I consider _____ much more interesting than _____.
b _____ is one of the most boring activities ever!
c I spend more time _____ than _____.
d I really should spend less time _____.

Cyber Tool

Record your answers at www.mailvu.com and send them to a classmate. Add extra details too. Any big differences?

3 Match three of a-f to the student's notes, then abbreviate the other three.

a 'The author states that the Internet is actually responsible for keeping people apart.'
b 'These days, more people send texts than ring.'
c 'Fathers and mothers seem to find less time to spend with their children.'
d 'Libraries have fewer customers now.'
e 'The book said four out of ten students cannot read when they finish primary school.'
f 'Playing games is the most common use of smartphones for the under-15 age group.'

Notes

○ 40% sts can't read when finish prim. sch.
○ net keeps ppl apart
○ parents spend less time w/ children

4 ▶ 7.12 Complete a-e with five of the 'point phrases'. Listen to check.

> point taken
> get to the point
> can I make a point?
> you have a point
> What's your point?
> that's exactly my point

a You said that already, but I still don't see what you mean.
  I don't get it. _____?
b I agree with you entirely. Actually, _____.
c Oh, OK—_____! I understand what you're trying to say now.
d I don't completely agree with you, but I think _____.
e Could you please _____? I have no idea what you're talking about.

5 Order the words to make 'discussion' phrases. Be careful, there's one extra word in each.

a by / of / what / depends / you / on / mean / it / …
b let / hold / on / finish / me / in / a / second / .
c that / can't / deny / to / we / …
d true, / that / be / is / may / but / …
e be / more / agree / I / couldn't / .
f totally / am / disagree / I / .

6 ▶ 7.13 Listen to six extracts from lesson 7.5 and number expressions a-f in 5 as you hear them.

7 Find the connection between the song line above and this lesson. Do the same with the other unit 7 song lines.

Can you remember…

▶ 10 parts of a car? SB→p. 73
▶ 5 words where acc = /aks/? SB→p. 73
▶ 8 phrasal verbs for machines? SB→p. 73
▶ 5 shopping advice words? SB→p. 74
▶ 2 collocations for say and 4 for tell? SB→p. 75
▶ 3 ways to ask someone to wait? SB→p. 76
▶ 7 verbs for using a computer? SB→p. 76
▶ 1 verb to report a command? SB→p. 79
▶ 1 verb to report a request? SB→p. 79
▶ 6 phrases for expressing your view? SB→p. 81

How important are looks?

8.1 | **8**

1 ▶ 8.1 Listen to a podcast. Who worries more about their looks, the man or the woman?

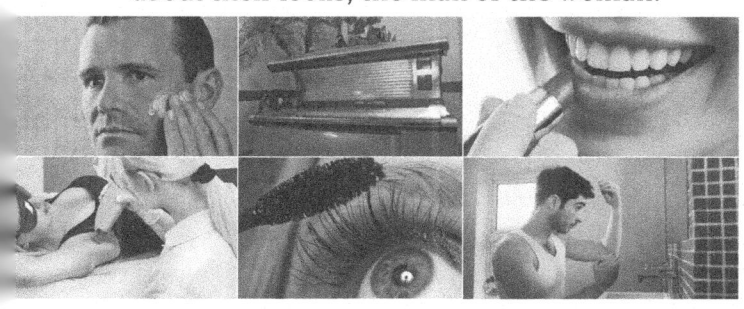

2 ▶ 8.1 Listen again and number the beauty items as you hear them, 1-6. Read the AS 8.1 on pp. 56-57 to check.

⏻ Cyber Tool

Record a 'podcast' about your beauty secrets and send it to a classmate. What products do you use?

3 Complete a-f with reflexive pronouns.

a My father accidentally hurt _____ when shaving.
b Some people are selfish. They only think of _____.
c When I was younger I considered _____ 'indestructible'.
d Jane has too little time to care much for _____.
e My girlfriend and I always enjoy _____ together.
f I love you more than I love life _____, my darling!

4 Complete the online advert with these verbs in the correct form.

| cut down | cut out | put on |
| stick to | take up | work out |

Wanna stop _____ weight? Wanna be healthy?
See a nutritionist about a planned diet and _____ it. That's the best way to _____ on food and _____ soft drinks altogether. In addition, _____ a physical activity and make sure you _____ every week!

5 (MAKE IT **PERSONAL**) Read the article. True (T) or false (F)? Which do you think would work best for dieters?

a In the banana diet, you have to eat bananas for every meal.
b Japan had to buy bananas from other countries.
c In the air diet you role-play the act of eating.
d The French magazine says the diet leads to anorexia.
e The baby food diet might work because you simply don't eat enough.
f The cookie diet is based on meal substitution.

Too far-out?

Do you really want to lose some pounds before next summer? Check out these bizarre ideas:

A The Morning Banana Diet, Japan

A pharmacist started this crazy diet back in 2008 to try and help her husband, who was experiencing weight problems. The diet is very easy to follow. Breakfast is a banana and a glass of water at room temperature. You can have anything for lunch and dinner, but you must be in bed by midnight. A popular singer who took up the diet gave an interview on TV and millions copied her. Sales of bananas immediately went up across the country, supermarkets sold out and Japan was forced to increase imports!

B The Air Diet, France

French women's magazine *Grazia* announced a new diet in February 2012: the 'air diet.' All you have to do is prepare any food you want, put it on a plate, get your knife and fork ready and then... stop. That's right, you do everything except actually eat. Doctors might call this anorexia, but the magazine insists it is a real diet. It also suggests a soup made of water and salt. Well, it's cheap and you won't put on weight by eating that!

C Kiddie Diets, USA

Hollywood is famous for its obsession with beauty, so it's no surprise that two of the craziest diets originated there: the baby food diet and the cookie diet.

In one you lose weight by eating like a 18-month child. The only things on the menu are pureed carrots and bananas, and absolutely nothing else.

In the other, dieters live on cookies, but not the average chocolate cookie. They're special low-calorie cookies with enough nutrients to replace normal meals and appetite suppressants to stop you getting hungry. Sounds delicious—but you'll still be eating like a child.

6 Correct the mistakes. Tick the three correct sentences.

a I look my older sister. We're both tall and fair.
b This looks like a nice spa.
c You look sad. Have you had some bad news?
d She's 45, but she looks like younger.
e Your new dress looks so fancy.
f Your brother looks a film star.

8.2 Do you like to hear gossip?

1 Match statements a-e to the responses.

a What was that loud bang? Was it a gun?
b Hank and Sue are late again.
c Kate still hasn't finished that report.
d Enzo didn't pass the exam.
e I arrived at the office at 4.30, but there was nobody there.

☐ Oh, she will. She can't have forgotten.
☐ They must have gone home early.
☐ They must have got lost again. They never take their satnav.
☐ No. It might have been a car or motorbike engine.
☐ Well, he can't have studied very hard.

2 ▶8.2 Complete a-e with **must've**, **might've** or **can't have** + the verbs below. Listen to check.

| be | come | oversleep | see | win |

a The thief _____ in through that window. Look—it's still open.
b **A** A woman answered the phone. I guess it was his wife.
  B It _____ his wife. She died last year.
c The players look so happy. They _____ the match.
d Janet is late today. She _____.
e You _____ my sister last week. She was working in China.

3 ▶8.3 Listen to these parents discussing their son, Gavin. Who's criticising and who's sympathising? What do you think the problem is?

4 ▶8.4 Listen to the second part to check and circle the correct form in a-e. Do their attitudes change?

a The father **likes** / **doesn't like** Gavin's friend.
b The mother thinks Gavin was **irresponsible** / **responsible**.
c The artist probably **asked** / **didn't ask** Gavin how old he was.
d The father **would** / **wouldn't** have preferred a dragon tattoo.
e The mother is probably **going** / **not going** to get a tattoo.

5 ▶8.5 Listen and write five extracts from the story. Listen again to check.

a I guess _____ it.
b It _____ weekend.
c He _____ himself.
d He _____ money.
e It _____ worse.

6 ▶8.6 Listen and rephrase with **must've**, **might've** or **can't have**. Follow the model.
  Model: Maybe he ate something bad.
  You: He might've eaten something bad.

Have you ever cut your own hair?

1 Read Sam's email and order these items as she mentions them, 1-3. Match each one to her feeling about it.

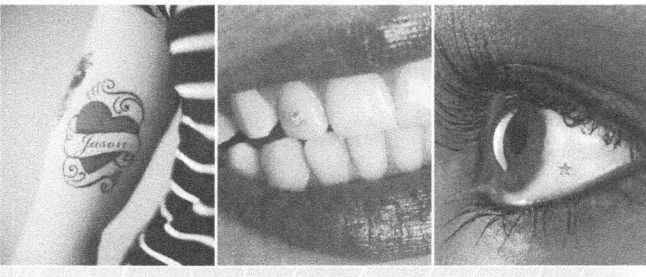

☐ too expensive   ☐ not available in the UK   ☐ did it but regrets it

Dear Ada,
Hope everything's OK with you.
Listen, I need your help! Can you ring me when you get this, please? Only you can understand what I'm going through now. You know Jason and I have been planning our wedding for ever. Ever since we got engaged last month I've been thinking about what to do to mark the date. Remember that eyeball jewel implant we saw in Amsterdam? I decided to have that, but I found out you can't get it done here. Can you believe it? Anyway, Jason gave me this gorgeous ring, so I decided to have a little diamond put into my front tooth to match it. But, wow, when I talked to the dentist, I realised I couldn't afford that, no way.
Well, to cut a long story short, last week I decided to get a tattoo on my arm—it's a red heart, with 'Jason' in the middle. I was surprised it didn't hurt more to be honest. But then, you'll never guess what happened on Saturday. Jason broke up with me. Really. Just like that! I think he's found somebody else, but he says he hasn't. We'll see. Anyway, now I just have to lose this tattoo. You're having yours removed with a laser, right? Should I do it now or wait a while? Please call me a.s.a.p.
xoxo,
Sam

2 ▶ 8.7 Write four sentences to summarise the information in 1. Listen and compare.

She wanted to speak to Ada, but sent her an email instead.
  a She wanted to get a jewel...
  b She thought of getting...
  c She got...
  d Now she...

3 Re-read. True (T), false (F) or don't know (D)?
  a Ada must be Sam's best friend.
  b Sam and Jason had been engaged for a long time.
  c Sam threw away Jason's ring.
  d The tattoo took ages to do.
  e Sam was expecting to split up with Jason.
  f Jason might have a new girlfriend.
  g Ada and Sam both have tattoos and want to laser them off.

4 ▶ 8.8 Sam is getting married to her new boyfriend. Listen and rephrase her sentences. Follow the model.

Model: I have my hair cut at the hairdresser's. Yesterday.
You: I had my hair cut at the hairdresser's yesterday.

5 Answer the questions in the **ID Task Manager** to find what you should do with tasks a-g and add three more of your own.
  a tidy / room
  b cut / hair
  c clean / something (what?)
  d redecorate / something (what?)
  e prepare dinner
  f manage your social network
  g fix / something (what?)

ID Task Manager

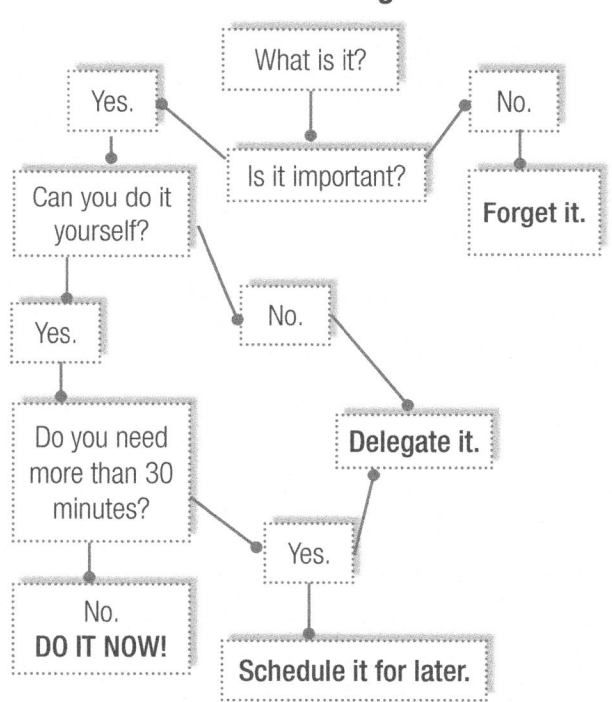

[Flowchart: What is it? → Is it important? → No: Forget it. / Yes: Can you do it yourself? → No: Delegate it. / Yes: Do you need more than 30 minutes? → No: DO IT NOW! / Yes: Schedule it for later.]

6 (MAKE IT **PERSONAL**) For each item in 5 you will delegate, make a statement like this:

I'm going to get my (teeth cleaned). I'll ask (my dentist) to do it.

Cyber Tool

1. Email your answers in 5 to a classmate. Can you help each other?
2. List six things you regularly get done by others and two you're proud of always doing yourself. Record and email it to a classmate. How many are the same?

8.4 Have you got a lot of furniture in your room?

1 Use the clues to complete the crossword.

Across
2 It's above you in any room. It rhymes with *feeling*.
5 It's what you put your head on in bed at night. It begins with *p*, and has two syllables.
6 You have one under you in bed. They're usually made of cotton. Rhymes with *feet*.
7 Most rooms have four of them. Rhymes with *ball*.
8 Rhymes with *door*. You walk on it, so it's the 'opposite' of 2 across.

Down
1 You usually have one on either side of a bed. Two words, the first begins with *b*, the second *t*.
3 You need this to see or read at night. Four letters, three of them consonants.
4 To keep warm in bed you need one of these, and / or a duvet. Two syllables, the first rhymes with *thank*.
9 A small carpet, usually next to a bed or near a fire. Rhymes with *mug*.

Cyber Tool
Record a description of your bedroom for a partner. Use all the words in the puzzle. Are your rooms similar?

2 Read the first paragraph of the following article and circle the correct alternative in a-c.
a **More / Fewer** people are living in cities.
b Flats in **a few / many** cities are getting smaller.
c Designers **are / aren't** adapting to the changes.

Modern Home DESIGN

The world is urbanising and, with more and more people living in a small space, we are seeing changes in the houses and flats we live in. One of the biggest, or should I say smallest, changes is in the size of our living space. Modern apartments, from New York to Tokyo and London to Rio, are getting increasingly smaller and therefore we are having to find interesting new ways to make everything fit. Here is our favourite space-saving design of the week.

The BedUp
At night it looks like any other _____, but when you wake up in the morning you can lift the _____ up so that it is suspended from the _____. Imagine the space you can save—4 m² to be exact. Under the _____ is a _____ so that you can work during the day. Small _____ in the bottom of the _____ give plenty of light so you can see what you are doing. At night you clear the top of your _____ and the _____ drops back to the _____, ready for you to climb in and go to sleep. Genius!
Read next week for more top designs!

3 Now read the second paragraph and complete with these words. You can use each word more than once.

> bed   ceiling   desk   floor   lamps

4 ▶8.9 Complete a-g with question tags. Listen to check and repeat. Pay attention to the intonation and mark the tags ↗ or ↘.

Random Question Generator
a You're not British, _____?
b It's hot today, _____?
c You like football, _____?
d You had an English lesson yesterday, _____?
e The teacher won't give a test this week, _____?
f You'll finish your homework soon, _____?
g You'd like a coffee now, _____?

5 ▶8.9 Listen again and record your answers.

6 ▶8.10 Listen, repeat and add the question tag. Follow the model.
Model: You haven't got much furniture in your bedroom.
You: You haven't got much furniture in your bedroom, have you?

Is your listening improving?

♪ And if you listen very hard, the tune will come to you at last, when all are one and one is all, to be a rock and not to roll. ♪ **8.5**

1 Read the article and match the headings to paragraphs a-d. There are two extra.

- Mix your methods
- Don't be afraid!
- More than the language
- Read a lot
- Open your ears
- Guessing is good

Four language learning hints

Learning a new foreign language is hard work—but there are things you can do to make it quicker and easier. Read on to find out.

a _____

We spend most of our 'communication time' listening, so this is obviously an essential skill to develop. But how? Living abroad is expensive and language classes don't always focus on listening. Well luckily for you, sound is all around you—from songs to streamed TV programmes to podcasts. All you need to do is find the time to put your headphones on. A little every day is best.

b _____

How you feel about the language is the key to progression. If you learn about the culture behind the language, you will understand more about the language itself, and feel more comfortable speaking with fluent speakers.

c _____

Sometimes we don't know exactly what a word means, even in our own language, and that is fine. In a foreign language this obviously happens more often, so learn to relax about it. Now, dictionaries are great and every language student should have one, but don't pick it up for every word you don't know. Instead, learn to focus on the words you know and trust your guesses for the ones you don't.

d _____

This is the most important tip of all. It doesn't matter how many conjugations you know or how much vocabulary you've studied. If you are paralysed with fear when you have to produce it, it is all a wasted effort. Everybody will be pleased that you are trying; the more you try, the better you'll feel, and the better you feel, the more you'll want to learn. So forget your insecurity. Hold your nose and jump in! Mistakes are learning opportunities. The more you speak, the quicker you will improve. So go for it!

---

2 Re-read and underline:

a three things to listen to.
b a problem with studying in another country.
c a way to feel better when talking to fluent speakers.
d advice for looking up words.
e two things that happen when you make an effort to speak.

3 ▶8.11 Add a suffix (*-ion*, *-ive*, *-ly*, *-ial*, *-able*, *-ity*) to form a word from the text, making the necessary changes. Mark the stress and listen to check.

a comfort_____
b communicate_____
c essence_____
d expense_____
e insecure_____
f obvious_____

4 ▶8.12 Complete the gaps with one word and correct one mistake in each comment. Listen to check.

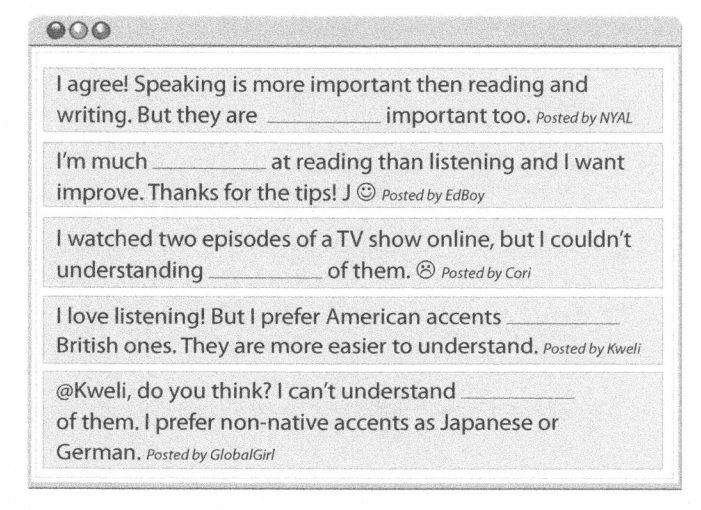

I agree! Speaking is more important then reading and writing. But they are _____ important too. *Posted by NYAL*

I'm much _____ at reading than listening and I want improve. Thanks for the tips! J ☺ *Posted by EdBoy*

I watched two episodes of a TV show online, but I couldn't understanding _____ of them. ☹ *Posted by Cori*

I love listening! But I prefer American accents _____ British ones. They are more easier to understand. *Posted by Kweli*

@Kweli, do you think? I can't understand _____ of them. I prefer non-native accents as Japanese or German. *Posted by GlobalGirl*

⏻ Cyber Tool

Which skill is / was the most difficult for you? Which is / was the easiest? What did you do to overcome the difficulties? Record your ideas and share with a classmate.

5 The song line on this page is obviously about the importance of listening hard. Find the connections between the four song lines and lessons in unit 8 of the Student's Book.

Can you remember...

- 6 phrasal verbs? SB→p. 83
- the 8 reflexive pronouns? SB→p. 83
- the difference between *must've*, *might've* and *can't have*? SB→p. 84
- 8 causatives with *have* and *get*? SB→p. 87
- 8 furniture words? SB→p. 88
- rules for question tags in ⊕ and ⊖ statements? SB→p. 89
- how intonation changes the function of question tags? SB→p. 89
- 3 tips for predicting information when listening? SB→p. 90

9.1 Does crime often worry you?

1 ▶9.1 Circle the word with the different underlined sound. Listen to check.

a a br<u>i</u>be	the pol<u>i</u>ce	a sp<u>ee</u>ding fine
b a cr<u>i</u>me	to k<u>i</u>dnap	v<u>i</u>olence
c organ<u>i</u>sed	p<u>i</u>racy	to go to pr<u>i</u>son
d a cred<u>i</u>t card	to st<u>ea</u>l	stat<u>i</u>stics

Cyber Tool

Create four sentences, a-d, by combining the three words each time. Record them and share with a classmate. Whose sentences are the most creative?

2 ▶9.2 Listen to extracts 1-4. How many times do you hear the sounds in the pictures?

1 l
2 s
3 w
4 θ

3 ▶9.2 Listen again and write the extracts down.

4 Complete the table. Mark the stress on the words you write.

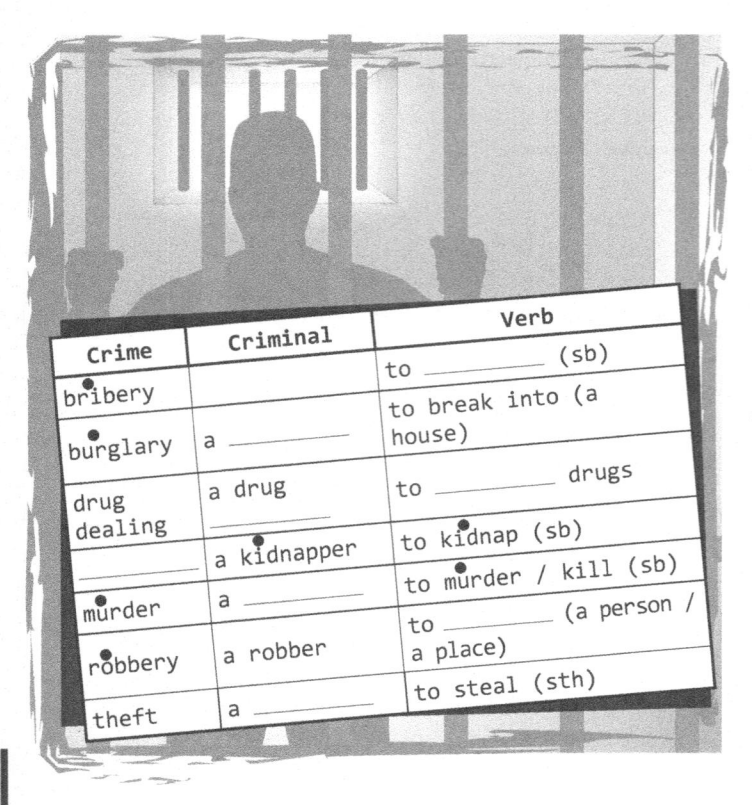

Crime	Criminal	Verb
bríbery		to _____ (sb)
búrglary	a _____	to break into (a house)
drug dealing	a drug _____	to _____ drugs
_____	a kidnapper	to kidnap (sb)
múrder	a _____	to murder / kill (sb)
róbbery	a robber	to _____ (a person / a place)
theft	a _____	to steal (sth)

5 Change the underlined words to rewrite a-f.

a In the film *Psycho*, Norman Bates <u>murders</u> travellers.
  In *Psycho*, the character Norman Bates is a <u>murderer</u>.

b A UN report says the number of Afghans paying <u>bribes</u> to teachers tripled between 2009 and 2012.
  _____ in education tripled over three years in Afghanistan, says the UN.

c <u>Kidnappers</u> have taken a local businessman and are demanding money.
  Criminals _____ a businessman and are holding him until they receive cash.

d The mafia is an international <u>criminal organisation</u>.
  The mafia is an international group that specialises in _____.

e Three men <u>robbed</u> the bank yesterday and got away with over £5,000.
  There was a _____ at the bank yesterday.

f The police are looking for a female suspect after the <u>theft</u> of a painting.
  The police are searching for a woman after she _____ a painting from a museum.

6 ▶9.3 Listen to a tour guide and answer a-d.

a Who is the man in the photo?
b Where did he live?
c Who was Herbert Hoover?
d Why did the man in the photo finally go to prison?

7 ▶9.4 Complete extracts a-d with the verbs in brackets in simple, continuous, perfect or perfect continuous. Listen to check.

a You _____ at the site of one of the most famous Chicago legends. (look)
b _____ you _____ who lived at the Lexington Hotel? (know)
c Oh yeah! I _____ about him. (hear)
d They arrested him because he _____ tax for many years on his illegal money. (not pay)

How could your city be improved quickly?

1 ▶9.5 Order the words in a-d to make sentences. Cross out one extra word in each. Listen to check.

a named / of / innovative / the / was / most / Medellín / world's / recently / city / .

b was / different / were / eight / judged / by / it / criteria / .

c and / created / communities / was / public / government / reached / spaces / were / programmes / these / .

d neighbourhood / by / a / considered / dangerous / once / this / was / slum / .

2 Read the web comments and mark them ⊕ positive or ⊖ negative.

What makes you proud of your city?

Isabel: My favourite singer, Shakira, _____ born here. *9 months ago*

Jed: Help! I _____ surrounded by idiots all the time. I need to get out of here! *11 months ago*

Caitlin: Well, I just love the Statue of Liberty. It _____ given by the French. *11 months ago*

Jose: We have a beautiful park that _____ filled with trees and birds. It's very peaceful. *1 year ago*

Donna: Er, let's see. There _____ the place… oh no, wait. How about all the… hang on. We have a great… nope, nothing. *1 year ago*

Simon: We have the world's first underground railway. It started in 1863—but it _____ updated a lot since then! *18 months ago*

3 Complete 2 with verb **be**. Which one is not passive voice?

Cyber Tool
Email or text a classmate saying what makes you proud of your city. Any similarities?

4 Read the article and match paragraphs a-c to the headings 1-4. There's one extra.

1 Global success ☐
2 Birth of a system ☐
3 Quality not quantity ☐
4 How it works ☐

URBAN MOBILITY

BRT system in Curitiba

a When the city of Curitiba, Brazil, hit one million inhabitants in the 1970s, it couldn't afford a $300-million underground system. So <u>somebody developed an alternative system</u>, the Bus Rapid Transit (BRT). Today, <u>people consider it</u> a success because it combines the speed of trains with the low cost of buses.

b <u>People often compare Curitiba's bus system</u> to an underground railway: exclusive lanes, pre-paid ticket counters, good quality stations and sensors that communicate with smart traffic lights. Today, <u>Curitiba's 2.3 million residents use its buses</u> to commute to work quickly and efficiently.

c <u>People have adopted the BRT system</u> in 83 cities worldwide, including Guangzhou, one of China's fastest-growing cities, and <u>the US government</u> will <u>soon implement it</u> in parts of Chicago.

5 Transform the underlined phrases in 4 to passive voice. Only use **by + agent of passive** if necessary.

6 ▶9.6 Transform what you hear into passive voice. Follow the model.

Model: *We have made a lot of progress.*
You: *A lot of progress has been made.*

9.3 Where will you be living in five years' time?

1 ▶9.7 Listen and number the phrases, 1-10, as you hear them.

- [2] Want to go?
- [ ] Do you think he'll have stopped smoking?
- [ ] We'll be working tomorrow.
- [ ] We love beans cooked by your mother.
- [ ] It will spread across the park.
- [1] One, two, go!
- [ ] Do you think he loved hot smoking?
- [ ] It will be working tomorrow.
- [ ] It will have been cooked by your mother.
- [ ] Wheels, spread across the park.

> **Cyber Tool**
> Record yourself on www.vocaroo.com saying 1-10. Compare with the original. Is your pronunciation similar?

2 Read the tips and cross out three sentences that **shouldn't** be in the article.

Stay Safe in Cyber Space

The boom in technology means that laptops, smartphones and tablets are everywhere. Unfortunately, so are the criminals who are trying to get inside them. Read our security tips to learn how to protect yourself from cybercrime.

Tip 1: Make sure your anti-virus software is **up-to-date**. Let it expire before you renew it. Hackers are creating new viruses all the time and only the very latest software can truly protect you.

Tip 2: Get a **tracking** app. Tablets and smartphones are the perfect **target** for thieves. Download a tracking app so the police can follow your device and find it.

Tip 3: Use strong **passwords**. Combinations of numbers and letters are a good idea. Add capital letters too, if you can. Try using your name and birthday—nobody will guess that! And don't use the same password for multiple accounts.

Tip 4: Click carefully. Don't **click** on links in emails and social networks, especially if you don't know where they came from.

Tip 5: Turn Wi-Fi off. If you can use your device as a Wi-Fi hotspot, protect it with a password and turn off the **hotspot** when you're not using it. Don't use the Internet at home. This will prevent other people signing in to your network.

3 Match the **bold** words in 2 to their definitions and examples a-f.

a _____ noun (C) an area with a lot of activity. A popular area. Usually two words but one when referring to the Internet. E.g.: *This area was a crime _____ a few years ago, but it's safe now.*

b _____ verb (-ing, -ed) to follow evidence. E.g.: *The hunters _____ the tiger through the forest.*

c _____ adj. very modern. E.g.: *The surgeons used _____ techniques.*

d _____ noun (C) a thing you want to get, attack or achieve. E.g.: *Our sales _____ is 500 units per month.*

e _____ noun (C) a word or phrase that lets you enter. E.g.: *You can't come in until you give me the _____.*

f _____ verb (-ing, -ed) select something on a computer screen by pressing a button. E.g.: *Use the mouse to _____ on the icon.*

4 Rewrite a-e using **by**.

a You can make your computer more secure if you use virus protection software.
b The last guests arrived just before 10pm.
c Some hackers uploaded the malware.
d Midnight is the latest I'll be home. I may get home before that.
e Tony improved a lot because he worked hard.

5 ▶9.8 Listen to two colleagues. True (T) or false (F)? Which man is Sam, A or B?

a Both men are looking forward to the weekend.
b Sam has to give his boss the report first thing on Monday.
c Sam is going to watch sport at the weekend.
d Sam likes the Lakers.

6 ▶9.8 Complete extracts a-d with three words in each. Listen again to check and repeat.

a I think I _____ all the way through.
b He just gave it to me and he _____ Monday.
c Hopefully _____ finished in time to watch the game.
d If the Lakers win, my prayers _____ answered.

7 Write ⊕ or ⊖ future sentences in 1-3 about Sam and Phil. Use the verbs given.

1 Sam _____ (have fun) this weekend.
2 Sam _____ (finish the report) Saturday evening.
3 Phil _____ (see his children) this weekend.

> **Cyber Tool**
> Record four or five sentences about your plans for next weekend and share them with a classmate. Whose weekend sounds better?

Have you ever been to court?

9.4

1. ▶9.9 Listen to two friends discussing a news story. Tick the correct headline.

   > 19-year-old arrested for illegal downloads: 13 GB found on disk
   > NY teen arrested for selling movie before official release date

2. ▶9.9 Listen again. True (T) or false (F)?
   a All of Peter's downloads were illegal.
   b He was sentenced to five years in prison.
   c He made lots of copies of the *Transformers 4* Blu-ray disc.
   d He made a lot of money selling those copies.

3. ▶9.10 Listen to the rest of the dialogue. What are their opinions? Write man (M), woman (W) or neither (N).
   He should:
   ☐ be acquitted   ☐ pay a fine   ☐ be sentenced to one year in prison
   ☐ do community service   ☐ be sentenced to life

4. Match the start of criminal biographies 1-2 to two of endings a-c.

   1. Adam Worth (1844-1902) was the original master criminal. At 17, he joined the American Union Army but was soon registered as 'killed in action', giving him the opportunity to begin his criminal career. In 1869, when detectives were tracking him after a bank robbery in Boston, he decided to move to Europe. From there, he organised crimes such as illegal gambling in Paris, diamond thefts in South Africa, art thefts in England and bank robberies in Belgium.

   2. Today he is known as Frank Abagnale Jr, but this is just one of nine identities he has used. Frank started by writing false paycheques for his various bank accounts. Then at 16, he decided to travel the world so he created an employee ID and pilot's licence and then phoned Pan Am airways claiming to be a pilot who had lost his uniform. With the right clothes, he flew around the world staying in five-star hotels and using fake cheques, a life that inspired the film *Catch Me If You Can*.

   a. French police eventually caught him, but 12 other countries also wanted to charge him with fraud. After a year in prison in France, he spent six months in a Swedish jail. Next he was returned to the USA, where he was sentenced to 12 years. After just five, the FBI approached him to work as a security consultant, a job that he still has today.

   b. He moved first to Australia and then to Brazil. Four years later, the police discovered where he was hiding, but by that time he'd had a son and could not be extradited. He stayed in Brazil for 31 years before returning voluntarily to the UK to face the rest of his 30-year sentence. He spent eight years in prison, but was released just before his 80th birthday.

   c. He earned the nickname 'the Napoleon of Crime' for his various criminal activities and was also the inspiration for the character Moriarty: Sherlock Holmes' criminal adversary. He was eventually caught for a robbery in Belgium and sentenced to seven years in prison, although he was released after four for good behaviour.

   Cyber Tool
   Use the Internet to discover the identity of the third criminal.

5. Re-read and answer a-f Adam Worth (A), Frank Abagnale Jr (F) or both (B).
   a Started committing crimes in his teens.
   b Is no longer alive.
   c Was an international criminal.
   d Was released early.
   e Used his criminal experience legally.
   f Had his life fictionalised.

6. ▶9.11 Listen and repeat the underlined extracts from 4. Notice the connections, schwas and silent letters.

7. (MAKE IT **PERSONAL**) Choose the correct preposition in a-e. Note your answers.
   a How much stress are you **under / with** at the moment?
   b Do you stop for a coffee **in / on** your way to work or school?
   c What is **in / on** the street corner near your house?
   d Have you ever waited more than an hour **for / to** a bus?
   e How many **from / of** your friends are the same age as you?

   Cyber Tool
   Record and share your answers with a classmate. Any surprises?

9.5 What was your best birthday present ever?

♪ Don't speak. I know what you're thinking. I don't need your reasons. Don't tell me... ♪

1 Read the headline and choose the best definition for the crime.

Man Charged with Arson After Cigars Catch Fire

a **arson**: *noun.* Smoking in public places.
b **arson**: *verb.* To play with fire.
c **arson:** *noun.* Burning something deliberately.

2 ▶9.12 Read and order the rest of the story, 1-5. Listen to check.

- ○ The insurance company refuses to pay the lawyer and he takes them to court. The judge decides that because the insurance company hadn't specified what kind of fire was unacceptable, they would have to pay.

- ○ The insurance company pays the lawyer but then… they have him arrested for arson, saying that he had deliberately burned his own property to claim the insurance money!

- ○ So, have you heard the story about the lawyer and the cigars? Here's how it goes.

- ○ About a month later he contacts the insurance company to ask for his money because his cigars have disappeared in 'a series of very small fires'.

- ○ A lawyer buys a box of very rare, expensive cigars. To protect them, he takes out an insurance policy so that if they are damaged he can receive some money.

3 ▶9.13 Listen to three dialogues and match the three excuse phrases you hear to the photos.

a Just hear me out.
b It's not what it looks like!
c It's not what you're thinking.
d It's not what it seems.
e I can explain.

4 ▶9.13 Listen again. True (T) or false (F)?

a Brad's computer had a problem and crashed.
b Brad's sorry for upsetting Yvette.
c Terry accepts responsibility for the kitchen.
d Terry's mother believes him.
e Leony's ex-boyfriend has sent her a text.
f Leony's sorry that Mark is upset.

5 ▶9.14 Look back and match lesson titles 9.1-9.5 to answers a-f. Listen to check and write down the follow-up question each time.

a ☐ Er… I don't know. I guess I'll still be living in this city somewhere.
b ☐ Not really, no. I try to make excuses, but people can usually guess from my face.
c ☐ No, of course I haven't!
d ☐ It doesn't really worry me too much. I live in a safe neighbourhood and I've never been a target.
e ☐ Well, one year I was in hospital because I'd broken my leg, and all my family and friends came to see me. We had a small, very quiet party.
f ☐ I guess it would be better if there was more public transport at night.

6 Find the connection between the song line on this page and the lesson. Do the same with the other four song lines in unit 9 of the Student's Book.

Can you remember...
- 7 crimes? SB→p. 94
- 4 verb aspects? SB→p. 95
- 3 uses for the word *by*? SB→p. 98
- 5 verb tenses to talk about the future? SB→p. 99
- 8 words for crime and punishment? SB→p. 100
- 12 phrases for giving excuses? SB→p. 103

What makes you angry?

10.1 **10**

1 Match anger quotes a-e. Which one suggests anger is positive?

a "Anger is never without reason, — You wouldn't like me when I'm angry." *David Banner*

b "When angry, count to four; — They just cry. But when they get angry, they **bring about** a change." *Malcom X*

c "People won't have time for you — but **seldom** with a good one." *Benjamin Franklin*

d "Don't make me angry. — when very angry, swear." *Mark Twain*

e "When people are sad, they don't do anything. — if you are always angry or **complaining**." *Stephen Hawking*

Cyber Tool
Share your favourite love, hate or anger quote with a classmate.

2 Match the **bold** words in 1 to their definitions.

_____ *adv.* not very often, rarely.
_____ *verb* make something happen.
_____ *verb* be negative about things.

3 ▶ 10.1 Match dialogues 1-3 to what has angered each person. There are two extra.
☐ bad drivers ☐ insincerity ☐ school ☐ weather ☐ work

4 ▶ 10.1 Listen again. True (T) or false (F)?

a The two men work together.
b Wet weather depresses both of them.
c The woman's driving.
d The man thinks she overreacted.
e The customer gave the cashier the exact money.
f The cashier annoyed both women.

5 ▶ 10.2 Listen and repeat a-e making the connections. Notice the silent letters.
a ups_and_downs
b little by little
c sick_and_tired_ of_it
d peace_and quiet
e again_and_again

6 ▶ 10.3 Listen to five short dialogues and, at the beep, write the correct number, 1-5, in 5.

10.2 Have you got any pet hates?

1 Read the web article about pet hates and add these headings. There is one extra.

> Car modifications   Chewing gum
> Eating on public transport
> Music in shops

Things I Could Happily Live Without

By Karen Kaye

Getting irritated by the noise, dirt or smell of an inconsiderate world? Here are the things I would prohibit to make life a whole lot more pleasant. Do you agree with me? Let's start a revolution!

1. _____
Extra loud speakers in the boot so we can all hear your terrible music—inconsiderate. Neon lights under the vehicle—what's the point? And those terrible, noisy, turbo engines—nobody needs to hear them. I would start my revolution by making these people take the bus!

2. _____
Have you ever seen a camel eating? This is what people look like when they put that horrible stuff in their mouths. And then, to make things even worse, nine times out of ten people stick it to seats, tables, bus windows or just drop it on the floor. Ban the stuff, just like they did in Singapore.

3. _____
And another thing: I'm fed up with smelling other peoples' dinner when I'm stuck on a bus or on the metro. It makes me feel sick! Not to mention the paper and plastic that people leave. And then there's the risk of injury if they drop their hot coffee on me. Water might be OK, but only on hot days and make sure you take your bottle with you!

2 Re-read the article and answer a–e.

a Which problem does Karen feel is dangerous?
b Which item is illegal in another country?
c Which problem does not cause litter?
d Which problem does Karen suggest a punishment for?
e Which problem causes Karen to have a physical reaction?

3 10.4 Complete the comments on the article with these verbs. Add a preposition if necessary. Listen to check and notice the /ŋ/ sounds.

> complain   listen   make   meet   stop   throw

Len 1 hour ago
If people showed a little more consideration, this city would be much nicer. We're all responsible _____ things better. Let's get out there and do it. No more gum! Viva the revolution!

Lady1 2 days ago
Don't you think there are bigger things to worry about? Poverty, crime, violence. _____ these problems should be the priority.

Crazyboy 2 days ago
Why don't you just stay at home and avoid _____ other people? Problem solved.

SamSame 3 days ago
Not _____ your rubbish in the bin is just laziness, there's no other excuse for it. It makes the city look really bad.

Kimbo7 3 days ago
Hey! I enjoy _____ to my music when I'm driving. It's better than hearing people like you complain all the time.

Fifi88 3 days ago
Instead _____ about people on the Internet, why don't you learn to be a little more tolerant?

4 Do the posts agree (A) or disagree (D) with the writer?

Cyber Tool

Post your opinion. Write a short response to the article or add your own 'pet hate'. Email it to a classmate.

5 10.5 Listen to five more comments for the web article and write five words in each gap.

@ Crazyboy
You _____. She's allowed to have her opinion.

@ Lady1
Sure, nice idea. But who's _____?
What can we do?

@ SamSame
Honestly, I'm _____ that.
When did a few pieces of paper hurt anybody?

@ Kimbo7
Come on, you've got to admit it.
She does _____.

@ Len
_____ improving the city, sure, but banning chewing gum? Don't you think that's a little extreme?

6 10.6 Listen and repeat. Notice the weak articles and prepositions.

How assertive are you?

1 Take our unit 10 preposition test. Complete the phrases in **bold** with a preposition.

TEST

a Being this explosive can **be bad** _____ **you**.

b He has no **sense** _____ **humour**.

c My dad's always **complaining** _____ getting up early.

d Tell her to **forget** _____ her ex-boyfriend.

e You're the **king / queen** _____ **cool**!

f What's your **excuse** _____ not doing your homework?

g I've heard a **rumour** _____ you.

2 Complete sentences a–c with an infinitive and a gerund phrase using the given words.

a stop / ask / directions
After driving for half an hour we realised we were lost, so we _____.
After we bought our satnav system we _____.

b try / open / door
My hotel room was so hot because the a/c was broken. I _____ and windows, but it made no difference.
The other day I locked my keys inside the car! I _____ with a paperclip, like in films, but it didn't work.

c remember / visit / grandparents
I must _____ this weekend. It's their 50th wedding anniversary.
Do you _____ when you were a child? What did you do there?

d stop / buy / milk
After work I _____ because I had run out of it at breakfast.
My wife and I _____ after the health scares. They said on the news that it was dangerous.

3 ▶ 10.7 Read the advert and circle the correct forms. Listen to check.

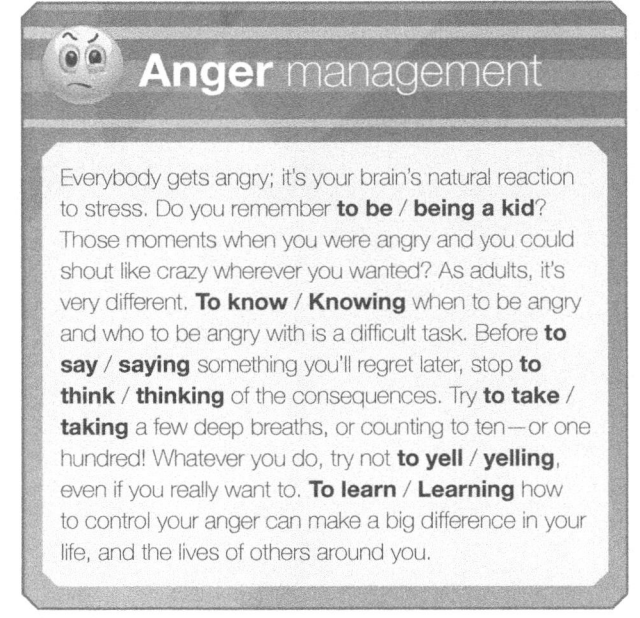

Anger management

Everybody gets angry; it's your brain's natural reaction to stress. Do you remember **to be / being a kid**? Those moments when you were angry and you could shout like crazy wherever you wanted? As adults, it's very different. **To know / Knowing** when to be angry and who to be angry with is a difficult task. Before **to say / saying** something you'll regret later, stop **to think / thinking** of the consequences. Try **to take / taking** a few deep breaths, or counting to ten—or one hundred! Whatever you do, try not **to yell / yelling**, even if you really want to. **To learn / Learning** how to control your anger can make a big difference in your life, and the lives of others around you.

4 *Tense review.* Complete the film review with the best form of the verbs in brackets.

Film Review

Dave Buznik, who _____ (play) by Adam Sandler, _____ (work) for a pet clothing company in NYC. He has trouble expressing his emotions and always keeps his anger under control. One day he is on a business trip and his anger finally _____ (explode). Dave goes to court and _____ (order) to take anger management therapy. We learn that he had _____ (humiliate) by a bully when he was a child—the bully pulled down Dave's pants when he _____ (try) to kiss the girl he liked. In the film, Dave slowly learns to express his anger.

5 ▶ 10.8 Listen to five situations and respond after the beep using a–e with infinitive or gerund.

a Why don't we stop (have) a break?

b I don't remember (put) them there.

c Have you tried (drink) some water?

d Could you please stop (do) that?

e Please, try (remember).

10.4 Would you say you were bossy?

1 ▶ 10.9 Listen to extracts a-e taken from lesson 10.4 in the Student's Book. How many words in each extract? Contractions count as two words.

a _____ b _____ c _____ d _____ e _____

2 ▶ 10.9 **Dictation.** Listen again and write them down.

3 Complete the leaflet with *yourself*, *themselves* or *myself*. Do you do any of these things?

Guide to Emotional Well-being

➡ Every day, repeat the phrase 'I like _____, I like _____. I love _____!'

➡ See _____ as others see you. You'll be surprised how positive the impression is.

➡ Understand that if someone is treating you badly, they probably don't like _____ either.

➡ Do _____ a favour. Learn to be independent. Get out and do things on your own.

➡ Accept that everybody doubts _____ sometimes. It's natural, but you can learn to beat it.

4 Study these extracts from ID 3. Match <u>phrasal verbs</u> a-j to the definitions.

a	Rachel's my next door neighbour. We <u>get on</u> really well.
b	The British <u>throw away</u> about five billion soft drink aluminium cans and bottles every year.
c	I would never be able to <u>give up</u> TV.
d	Drink or smoke here and you'll <u>end up</u> in jail!
e	I'll <u>get round to</u> doing the washing up later. Maybe after this TV programme.
f	Never <u>put off</u> until tomorrow what you can do the day after tomorrow.
g	As Jacob <u>grew up</u>, his parents realised he was gifted.
h	John Smith <u>ran out of</u> money.
i	And then he <u>got into</u> debt.
j	If this sounds familiar, <u>wise up</u>! Make a shopping list.

☐ postpone / delay a task
☐ arrive at a final point after a series of events
☐ discard, get rid of
☐ learn the truth
☐ have a good relationship
☐ do a task after waiting for some time
☐ use the final piece
☐ enter a place or situation
☐ become an adult / mature
☐ stop doing / using

5 ▶ 10.10 **Intuitive quiz!** Match a-j to the responses and complete with phrasal verbs from 4 plus **it** or **X** (no object). Use your intuition! Listen to check. How good were your guesses?

a Did you _____ in this city?
b Have you got today's newspaper?
c Have you uploaded your holiday photos yet?
d You know, biting your fingernails is a really bad habit.
e Er, Jim? I've got a little problem with the police.
f Have we got any orange juice left in the fridge?
g Hank hasn't returned any of my calls and...
h That sounds like a bad cough. Did you see a doctor about it?
i So lunch was... a bottle of cola, a doughnut and...
j Do you know Clara?

☐ No, we _____ last night.
☐ Wait! I've heard enough. Seriously, if you continue to eat like that you'll _____ losing your teeth, or worse.
☐ Yeah, I know. I should try to _____.
☐ Of course I do. We _____ great. We've known each other for years.
☐ Sue, you need to _____. Seriously, that guy is bad news.
☐ No, not yet. I guess I shouldn't _____ any longer. I'll make an appointment tomorrow.
☐ No, I moved here when I was 21.
☐ Oh, sorry, I _____ after I read it.
☐ No, I haven't _____ yet. I'll do it tomorrow.
☐ Well, don't come to me! You _____, you can get yourself out of it!

6 ▶ 10.11 Listen again and say the correct response after the beep.

What's your most common mistake in English?

♪... all I know is you're my favorite mistake. You're my favorite mistake.♪ **10.5**

1. Match the mistake quotes. Tick your favourite.

   a. Learn from the mistakes of others. You…
   b. Don't be afraid of making mistakes. Be…
   c. Everyone makes mistakes. The wise are not…
   d. Anyone who has never made a…
   e. The greatest mistake you can make in…
   f. Nothing that is worth…

   ☐ those who never make mistakes, but those who forgive themselves and learn from their mistakes. *Ajahn Brahm*
   ☐ mistake has never tried anything new. *Albert Einstein*
   ☐ can't live long enough to make them all yourself. *Eleanor Roosevelt*
   ☐ learning can be taught. *Oscar Wilde*
   ☐ afraid of not learning from them. *Anonymous*
   ☐ life is to be continually fearing you will make one. *Elbert Hubbard*

2. ▶ 10.12 Proofread and correct students' sentences a-j. Four have no mistakes; the others have two mistakes each. Listen to a teacher giving the class feedback to check. How many did you get right?

   a. I told to her it is difficult and asked her to help me.
   b. A lot new hotels are building in my city.
   c. It started raining soon after we left the house.
   d. My dad complains to get up early in the morning.
   e. I can't remember where is the my car.
   f. Where did you get your eyes checked?
   g. Can you tell me who wrote this song?
   h. How long are you living this city?
   i. He was awarded an Oscar for his role in the movie.
   j. She works like a secretary for a company who specialises in import / export.

3. Choose the correct alternatives in the poster.

   Our strengths and weaknesses in English
   1. I **think / find** it easy **to read / read** in English, but a little boring.
   2. I'm not so good **to remember / at remembering** new words.
   3. I have a lot of **difficulty / difficult** pronouncing 'sh' and 'ch'.
   4. **To listen / Listening** is very hard.
   5. **It's / Is** difficult to speak without pausing a lot.

4. ▶ 10.13 Give advice to students 1-5 in 3. Put the <u>verbs</u> in the correct form. Listen to five student-teacher dialogues to check.

   a. A good way of <u>improve</u> your pronunciation <u>be</u> <u>record</u> yourself.
   b. Try <u>focus</u> on the stressed words.
   c. How about <u>learn</u> some common phrases like 'I mean' or 'you know'?
   d. You should <u>consider</u> <u>read</u> things you <u>be</u> interested in.
   e. Have you <u>think</u> about <u>keep</u> a notebook for new words?

5. Look back through Student's Book units 6-10 and choose:

Page number:	Reason you chose this one?
The most interesting reading text.	
The best song line.	
The most difficult grammar point.	
The funniest cartoon in the grammar section (pp. 116-135).	
The most enjoyable listening / video.	

   Cyber Tool
   Record your answers at www.mailvu.com. Share them with a classmate.

6. Find the connection between the song line above and the language of this lesson. Do the same with the other four song lines in unit 10 of the Student's Book.

   Can you remember…
   - 8 mood words? SB → p. 104
   - 6 binomial phrases? SB → p. 105
   - 4 verbs followed by a gerund? SB → p. 106
   - 4 words / phrases followed by *for*? SB → p. 107
   - 4 words / phrases followed by *of*? SB → p. 107
   - 3 verbs with a different meaning when followed by an infinitive or a gerund? SB → p. 109
   - 6 phrasal verbs? SB → p. 111
   - 4 phrases to describe strengths and weaknesses? SB → p. 112
   - 6 phrases for making recommendations? SB → p. 113

Audio Script

Unit 1

▶ 1.7

In 2010, an American chat show host called Jimmy Kimmel invented a holiday which has become known as 'International UnFriend Day' for Facebook. He chose the 17th of November as the day each year to 'unfriend' or delete all of the Facebook friends who annoy you and aren't really your friends. He provides many examples of what does and does not constitute a real friend, and recommends removing family members and ex-boyfriends or -girlfriends immediately. A good test for whether or not they should stay or go is to ask yourself whether you would lend them money, if you've seen them within the past two years or if they would help you move house. If the answer to any of those questions is 'no', you should unfriend them on the 17th of November.

Kimmel points out that many people have hundreds, even thousands, of Facebook 'friends' and that it's impossible for all of them to be *true* friends, which actually cheapens your real relationships. He says unfriending on a specific day makes the act less hostile. You could post something to say you are removing anyone you haven't seen in the last year or two, for instance, or ask anyone who wants to stay on your page to post a comment.

▶ 1.8

a We've only just met. She seems nice.
b We've known each other for many years. We get on really well.
c We drifted apart for a few months this year, but now we text each other many times a day and go out every weekend. I know I can rely on J J.
d His name is Rob. Or Bob? I think.
e I haven't seen Joe in forever, but we email from time to time and I'm going to invite him to my wedding next month. It'll be good to see him again.
f Amy and I have a lot of fun together when we meet. Er, we're going out on Saturday for some pizza and gossip. I haven't seen her for a while, so we'll have a lot to talk about.

▶ 1.9

Mmmmhhh, OK. A: 'Does this person give you intense looks?' Wow, he does too! B: He doesn't hug me that often. Well, not more than other people. Huh! OK... Now, C: 'Have you spent more time together lately?' Have we? Er... No, not really. I wish! Next, D: 'Is your heart beating faster as you answer these questions?' Can't everybody hear it? Faster and louder! Fine. E: 'Do you spend more time with this person than with other friends?' Hmmm. I don't really. I don't... spend that much time with him. No. OK. F: I do! I do, I do! I love to talk before we go to bed. Now, G: 'I'm jealous of... everyone! Hope he is too, but... who knows, right? H: 'Are you going on holiday together any time soon?' Sadly no. That's it. Let's see what it says here...

▶ 1.14

B = Ben   M = Matthew

B I just couldn't finish reading *Antony and Cleopatra*. All those difficult words, mate.
M OK, here's the idiots' summary of the play. Caesar, Antony and Lepidus rule the Roman Empire.
B The three guys, right?
M Hmm, so Antony is married to Flavia...
B You mean Fulvia, right?
M Er, yeah. Fulvia. So Antony is married to Fulvia, but they don't get on very well. She lives in Rome, he lives in Alexandria, in Egypt, and cheats on his wife with Cleopatra, Queen of Egypt.
B Right! Antony and Cleopatra hang out together in Egypt.
M Then Antony's wife, Fulvia, dies and he goes back to help Caesar fight the enemies of Rome.
B Then Antony and Caesar's sister get married. What's her name?
M Octavia. Right. But they soon drift apart and Antony goes back to Egypt and Cleopatra.
B I bet Caesar didn't like that!
M He definitely didn't like it at all. So Caesar and Antony fall out and start to fight for control of Egypt.
B What happened in the end?
M Antony heard false news of Cleopatra's death and killed himself. When Cleopatra heard the love of her life was dead, she committed suicide too...
B ... with small black poisonous snakes. Got it! Thanks a lot, mate.

Unit 2

▶ 2.5

M = Mikaela   L = Lucy

M So, Lucy, which of these do you think is worse?
L That's a tough one. Erm... Well, I guess maybe floods. They caused a lot of damage in the city last year.
M Well, yeah, but, you know... my house wasn't damaged. And your house was OK too, so...
L Well that's not really the point. I mean, it caused a lot of problems for other people, and, for example, the government still hasn't fixed the old bridge. We still can't use it.
M Yeah OK, OK. But what about food? I mean the guys in the north have been waiting, what, three, four months for the rain and, you know, all the land is dry and...
L That's true. But, you know, I think we can solve that problem. Look, I mean, the Earth is something like 80% water and...
M Yeah, OK, but most of that is salt water or ice. You know, we can't just put the ocean on the desert and solve the problem, I mean, that's crazy.
L Ah! Well, that's where you're wrong. Scientists have been working on this and in, like, Israel I think, yeah, in Israel they've been using water from the oceans for many, many years.
M Really? Huh. That's interesting.
L Yeah, so you see, our problem isn't lack of water, like in a drought, it's really having too much water, like in a flood. So, if you look at it like that, floods are a bigger problem. And, you know, a lot of flooding problems are made worse by deforestation and global warming so, you know, there are things we can do to help stop flooding and...

▶ 2.9

A = answering machine   C = Cal

1 A Work 24/7! Finding jobs for you whatever you do. Please press one to speak to an expert. Press two... The expert is busy right now. Please leave a message.
  C Hello, Mr Connie. It's Cal Taylor here. I don't know if you remember me. I came in for an interview a couple of weeks ago. Erm, I'm looking for a job, er, any job and... Well, look, it's been two weeks and I haven't heard anything from you, or from any potential employers. Your website guaranteed I would only wait a week. I'm going to come into the office tomorrow and I want to talk about this with somebody. Goodbye.

A = answering machine   M = Mia

2 A Hello. You've reached the offices of Grabowsky and Loewe, specialists in career advice. We apologise that there is nobody to take your call right now, so please leave a message after the tone.
  M Hi, Ms Grabowky? Mia Stromboli here. You gave me your card at the conference in Seattle last Thursday. I'd like to arrange an appointment to discuss my career with you at some point. Er, a little about me. I've been working in the oil industry for 17 years now, both overseas and in the US. Erm, I have a lot of management experience and erm... Well, maybe I should tell you this when we meet. So, er, please call me back on 736-555-8191. Look forward to hearing from you. Bye.

A = answering machine   J = Jake

3 A Welcome to Five Star Chinese courses for professionals. Please press one to order your copy of our book. Press two for a quick language test. Press three to leave a message.
  J Hello? Hello. Yes, er... Look, I ordered a copy of *Selling in China for Beginners* and, er, it hasn't arrived yet. Er, the order number was, er... Let's see... It was SCB3020. Now, I checked... Oh, my name is Jake Powers. Now, look, I checked my bank account and I paid five weeks ago, so I've been waiting, for 35 days. Even with 28 days for delivery, the package is still a week late. Now, I know there were no promises about the mail, but this really isn't good enough. Now, you have my contact details and I want you to call me back before the end of the day so we can figure this out. OK?

▶ 2.10

G = guide   T = tourist   Z = zoo owner

1 G Oh my goodness! Look! There in front of us. I haven't seen one of those for years; they are extremely rare. Oh, isn't he amazing?
  T Is that a... is that... Oh gee! Martha, pass the camera, I'm going to take a photograph.
  G No! Don't open the door. Stay in the Jeep. We are safe in here, he thinks we are one big animal, just like him. If you get out, he might attack you. He can run faster than you think, and that thing on his nose isn't just for decoration.
2 G Shhh! We have to stay very quiet. Just 20 feet in front of me, and up in the trees. I can see... I can see that they're eating fruit, and I don't think they know we're here. Ah! These beautiful golden animals! They are very much at home here in the Brazilian Atlantic forest.
3 Z Hello, and welcome to Zoo Atlanta. Er, I know you're all very anxious to meet our new arrivals, but, er, first I'd like to take this, er, this opportunity to thank our colleagues in China. We have worked very closely with them over a number of years to, er, to protect this iconic species and to, er, to reach this success. The mother, Lun Lun, is doing very well and so are the twins.
4 G From our position, here in the helicopter, we can look down and see a fantastic sight. Mother and child travelling along next to each other, completely unaware of us, flying above them. These two will continue their migration along the eastern coast of the United States, from the warm waters in the south to cold feeding grounds of the north.

2.14

M = man W = woman

1 M Oh, I can't believe it! Another 'no' letter. This must be the fifth job this month. I'm never going to get a job as a journalist!
  W Hey, listen. You have to believe in yourself. Work hard and you'll get there. I know you can do it!
  M Huh. That's easy for you to say.

2 W Oh, here's my paycheque! Yeah! I've almost saved enough money for my trip!
  M Your trip? What are you talking about?
  W Duh! I've been talking about it, like, forever! Hannah and I are going to take a gap year. We're going to go backpacking and camping across the country and…
  M Wait a minute. You and *Hannah*? Hannah that can't stand spiders? That Hannah? Do you really think that's a good idea?
  W Oh come on, she's not that bad. And anyway, it'll be fun.

Unit 3

3.4

a Hi! This is your travel host, Naomi.
b I'd like to show you the top ten attractions of Madrid, Spain.
c Number ten, Plaza de Cibeles. Madrid is known for many beautiful squares like this one.
d The Cibeles fountain is an important symbol of this city.
e Number nine. Almudena Cathedral. It took more than a hundred years to complete its construction in 1993.
f The original site was occupied by Madrid's first mosque.

3.8

a The honking went on for hours until we slowly started moving.
b The firemen finally opened the door and helped each one of us up to the 15th floor.
c I walked out in my pyjamas to get the paper and the wind blew the door shut behind me.
d When we got back to the car park, I realised I'd left the keys somewhere.
e Almost 12 hours to buy tickets for a show sounds crazy, doesn't it?
f We couldn't get out because we were between stations.
g The observation deck was so full with people we couldn't get to the door to get down again.

Unit 4

4.1

R = Ruth D = Dan P = Phyllis

R I'm reading this fabulous book about 21st century skills.
D Not another book telling us to teach children collaboration and creativity, is it?
R Yes, among other important skills. It's a collection of papers by 21 different authors.
D Do any of the authors tell us how to motivate children to learn reading, writing and arithmetic these days?
R Well, Dan, children need much more than that to succeed in the 21st century. People need to be able to work together well to solve really complex problems, to show initiative and come up with ideas that have value to others, you know, being creative. Reading, writing and maths are just tools.
D It's all very well for theorists to say that, but how do you keep a group of teenagers engaged in a classroom these days? When everybody is texting everybody, or checking their Facebook timeline, or even gaming during classroom time?
R Precisely! Everyone's connected to technology and, suddenly, that has to stop the moment they enter a classroom. It's not natural! I really think we're right to use as much information technology in our schools as possible. That's how we prepare children for a future we can't even imagine. Let them use their mobile phones to learn. Let them look for information on the web and share it with everyone in class.
D Let them use their mobile phones in class? You can't be serious! How do you know they're not texting their friends?
P Frankly, Dan… Because you negotiate the rules with your students from the start.
D Fine, let's say they do use their smartphones to look up information for a project. You know as well as I do that the Internet is full of rubbish.
R Well, then you teach them how to find information they can trust. That's a 21st century skill.

4.2

R = Ruth D = Dan C = colleague

P = Phyllis

a R I think schools need to teach 21st century skills.
  P Do you think so? I mean, they learn those things at home. School is where they should learn what they can't learn in other places. So, no, I don't agree with you.
b D I believe we should concentrate on reading, writing and arithmetic.
  P I don't think so. Well, not only those things. What about art, or history, or music?
c R I think children have to learn how to solve problems creatively.
  D No, I don't think so. They should learn rules, rules, rules.
d R In my opinion, smartphones can be a useful learning tool in class.
  P Yeah, you're right. I use them all the time.
e D Smartphones shouldn't be allowed in class.
  C Oh, I think so too. They really annoy me. All that beeping.
f D I don't think students should look for information online. It's useless.
  R Oh, come on! You realy think that? The Internet is part of our lives now.
g R Teachers should teach students to find information on the Internet that they can trust.
  P That's absolutely right! Yes, I completely agree with you!

Unit 5

5.1

1 I bought a new pair of jeans last week. Do you like them?
2 That's a nice pair of sunglasses. Where did you get them?
3 I really want to buy some new sandals. Where can I get some?
4 So you gave your girlfriend some jewellery for her birthday. Did she like it?
5 I need a suit for my job interview. Where can I get one?
6 I bought a new T-shirt online. Do you like it?

5.2

A = Andreas J = Jia

A My bank manager has just approved a 2,000-pound loan for me.
J I thought you'd applied for three grand.
A I did, but they only approved two grand. I only make 500 quid a week, you know.
J Did your brother agree to be your guarantor?
A Nope. The good news is my dad agreed.
J Good for him. Do you pay very high interest on the loan?
A 8 per cent. I guess it's the standard rate for a three-year loan.
J Depends on the terms. When's your first payment due?
A The first of July.
J Will you be able to pay it off?
A I certainly hope so.

5.6

1 Ladies and gentlemen, we continue boarding American Airlines flight 542 with service to London through gate 37. At this time, we're ready to board passengers in group C. All other passengers, please remain seated. We'd like to invite passengers with 'group C' on their boarding passes to board now through gate 37. Please, have your boarding passes ready and passports open at the picture page.

2 Directors, teachers, fellow classmates and families and friends, we are the graduating class of 2014! It is a great honour to be here to commemorate this major moment in my life and that of my fellow classmates. I think we've all been looking forward to today as our prize for the hard work of the last four years.

N = narrator D = David

3 N In five, four, three, two, one. Ladies and gentlemen, from the top of New York's beautiful Rockefeller Center, we present the *David Perlman Show*. Please welcome your host: David Perlman.
  D Good evening, everybody. We have a great show for you tonight. Beautiful Miss Taylor Swift and Academy Award Winner Jennifer Lawrence are here, ladies and gentlemen.

5.10

C = customer S = shop assistant

C I bought this flash drive yesterday and realised it's only 64 GB instead of the 256 GB I paid for. Can I exchange it for the 256 GB?
S I just need to see your receipt, please.
C That's the thing. I threw it away, you see.
S In that case, I'm afraid there's nothing I can do.
C Seriously? But look, I have the bag.

5.12

C = customer S = shop assistant

C I like these shoes. Can I try them on?
S Sure. What size do you wear?
C Size 12.
S I'm sorry. We're sold out.
C Do you have the same shoe in brown?
S A size 12 in brown, right?
C Yep. Wait! Forget it. I'm really late as it is. Thanks.
S You're welcome, sir. Goodbye.
C Goodbye.

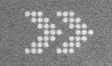

Unit 6

6.2

M = man   W = woman

1. M It's the first thing I watch in the morning and the last thing I watch at night. I have to know what's happening in the world.
   W Well, I just go online; there is so much information on there that I don't need traditional news programmes now.
2. W Yep, same time every day. I love it. All that drama, the hair and the heavy make-up. Some are very good too. Great acting, great screenplays and beautiful locations.
   M Great acting? You must be joking! No way! I have no patience for soaps. The TV networks show them instead of my team - it really annoys me. I love watching my team play.
3. M I'm voting for Jamal; he's pretty awesome on the stage.
   W Totally. Yeah, great voice, but the judges are giving him a hard time.
4. M Love them all, you know? Old episodes of *House*, *Grey's Anatomy*, you name it.
   W Yep, me too. Weird, though. We're not even doctors.
5. W Can't stand Letterman. Don't like the acid humour. I love Ellen, though… Ellen DeGeneres?
   M Nope. Never watched Ellen, but come on, Letterman's hilarious.

6.7

Warning!
There is a dangerous virus going around. It's called WORK.
If you receive WORK from your colleagues, boss, or anyone else, via email or any other means, DON'T TOUCH IT UNDER ANY CIRCUMSTANCES!
This virus will destroy your private life completely. If you come into contact with WORK, put on your jacket, take two good friends and get out.
The only antidote is known as EN-TER-TAIN-MENT. You can find it in theatres, clubs and cinemas. Take the antidote repeatedly until WORK has been completely eliminated from your system.
Forward this warning immediately to at least five friends. If you realise that you do not have five friends, this means that you are already infected and that WORK already controls your life.
Remember! It is a deadly virus!

6.10

L = Lynn   D = Djamilla

L Hi, Djamilla. Hey, I've just been reading a list of things artists want in their dressing rooms, you know, when they perform. They are crazy!
D Yeah! Any good ones?
L Loads. Guess what Beyoncé wants?
D No idea. Flowers, diet cola, a huge bath…
L No, Bey wants really juicy baked chicken, with fresh garlic, salt, black pepper and cayenne pepper, you know?
D No way! Like really hot chicken? Maybe it's good for her voice.
L Yeah. Hot babe Bey eats really hot chicken in the dressing room.
D Well, I heard Katy Perry wants a really specific list of crazy stuff.
L Oooohhh! What does California girl want in her dressing room?
D She wants like… a modern, glass top dressing room table and er… a pair of really ornate French orange floor lamps.
L You must be joking! A pair of ornate French lamps!!!
D I know, how mad is that?
L Shhhhhhh. Listen. I heard Britney Spears used to demand a framed photo of Lady Diana… mphhhhhh.
D What? You can't be serious. A photo of Lady Diana?
L I swear it's true. Well, at least that's what I heard. Bizarre, right? But not everybody is that mad. I mean, RiRi only wants Oreo cookies, nothing fancy.
D RiRi? Who's that?
L What! You don't know? That's Rihanna!
D Oh, right! RiRi, cool! So, she only wants biscuits? That's sweet.
L I know, right. I guess she can't live without them!
D 'It takes me all the way. I want you to staaaay!'
L Whoo! And you know Adele? She insists that anyone who gets free tickets for her shows has to make a donation to a charity.
D Wow. Free tickets. I wish! I'd love to see Adele. She's amazing.
L Yeah… That would be just great.

Unit 7

7.1

M = man   W = woman

Part 1 W … I have six children, two dogs and do a lot of shopping. That's why I must have a car with a really big [beep].
M OK, I'll open it so you can check for yourself.

Part 2 W Oh, no, no. I couldn't possibly deal with three pedals! It's hard enough with just the accelerator and the brake. I have absolutely no idea what to do with the [beep]. I need an automatic car.
M OK!

Part 3 W Er… I don't like this. These [beep] are extremely noisy, aren't they?
M Yes, I agree, madam. I'll change them for you.

Part 4 W Now could you open the [beep] so I can have a look at the engine?
M Sure. There you go. It's three cylinders but it's really powerful.
W Yes, it's, er, very, er, pretty…

Part 5 M This might be perfect for you. What do you think?
W Yes, I guess it is. It's so light! I can move it with one finger! Look, turning right, now turning left. Oh, this is the [beep] of my dreams!

7.6

M = Mr Keller   W = woman

W … Sure! How can I help you?
M Well, I need to know how to upload music from my computer to my tablet.
W OK. Let's see if I can help you. Er… First of all, can you tell me what kind of tablet you have?
M Yes. It's an iPad.
W OK. I wonder if you've installed iTunes on your computer?
M I what? I have no idea what you're talking about, Janet… I'm not really familiar with software names.
W Oh, dear. Never mind… Er… Do you at least know if you have a Mac or a PC?
M Yes, that I can tell you. I have a MacBook.
W Good, Greg! So you do have iTunes after all! Phew!
M Whatever. Maybe you could now tell me how I can upload music to my tablet?
W Yes, of course, you just…

7.10

A = Andy   J = Joe

A Hey Joe, have you seen my blog post?
J No. What's it about?
A Oh, it's basically just a list of all the dumb people that phone me up.
J Oh, yeah? Like what?
A Well, there was this guy the other day. He rang and said he was trying to connect to the Internet with our CD but it didn't work. And he asked what he was doing wrong.
J OK, so what's dumb about that?
A Well, I asked him what sort of computer he was using and he said he didn't have one, the CD was in the CD player!
J No way! That's ridiculous!
A I know, mad, right? And then there was this woman. I told her to press any key to continue and she paused for a while, thinking, and then said she couldn't find the 'Any' key.
J The 'Any' key! You must be joking!
A I know mate, I get it all the time. There was this one guy. I told him to click on 'My Computer', you know, the folder, right?
J Sure, of course.
A Yeah, well, he told me he couldn't see my computer, he could only see his computer!
J Are you serious? That's incredible.
A OK, how about this one: this guy rang up and said he'd like some help setting up his printer, so I asked him to connect his printer to his computer. And do you know what he said?
J Go on.
A He asked if he had to have his computer there! Like he was surprised, you know. I mean, how are you going to print without a computer?
J No way! Where do you find these people?
A I know mate, it's hard to believe. Oh, wait a minute, I didn't tell you the best one yet.
J Oh no! It gets worse?
A Oh yeah! This woman phoned and said she needed help installing Microsoft Office. So I told her to insert the disk.
J Right?
A Yeah, and she was like 'What? What disk?'.
J She didn't have a disk?
A Well, I asked her if she had bought Microsoft Office and she was like 'Oh… er… no. Did I have to buy it?'
J She didn't buy it and she phoned you for help? Some people are insane!

Unit 8

8.1

M = man   W = woman

M What do I do? Let's say that I didn't use to care much about my looks, but now there are so many products specifically designed for men that, er… Well, I'd been to the tanning salon so often that two months ago I decided to buy a tanning bed for the house. I know there can be some health issues with it but, er… I'm careful, you know. I don't spend all day in there or anything, just enough to give me a healthy natural colour. Er… What else? Oh, I'm almost done with the laser hair removal treatment. They are working on my facial hair now so… five more sessions and it's finished. Does it hurt? Oh, maybe a little, but it's worth it; I have much smoother skin now, no beard or chest hair. I like it. I use some products, like moisturiser, just to give me that healthier look, oh, and, and… a special hair gel. I get a manicure and pedicure twice a month, which for me is also a health matter too. My wife likes it; I guess she's the one who's inspired me, 'cause she's always taken good care of herself.

W Hmm… I have to admit I don't do much. If I followed every piece of advice I find in beauty magazines, then I'd be a lot poorer! Anyhow, I don't really like mascara or make-up! Ugh, I just think it's too much on my face. I obviously wear a good lipstick, and that's all. Maybe when I get older I'll rethink that, but for now I buy a good shampoo and conditioner and a special soap. Yeah, that's as far as I go. I'm happy when I look at myself in the mirror, but my friends are always trying to get me to wear more make-up, or, you know, try some new skin treatment. Not for me, not yet anyway…

8.4

F = father   M = mother

M Now, hang on a minute. He might've decided to do it himself. We don't know that Chris persuaded him.
F Oh, come on! You know what that boy's like.
M No, be fair. He must've been planning this for a long time. I mean, tattoos are expensive. He must've saved up a lot of money for it. And that's a good learning experience, you know, and… kind of responsible if you think about it.
F Hmmm. Still, the tattoo artist should have asked for ID or something, I mean, he's 16! Isn't that illegal or something?
M Yeah, but what's done is done. And actually… It is kind of sweet: 'I love Mom'.
F True, it could've been a lot worse, like a dragon or something.
M You know what? I think I might get one too—'I love Gavin'.
F You must be joking!
M Yeah, don't worry.

Unit 9

9.3

G = guide   T = tourist

G Welcome to Chicago City Crime Bus Tour. Today, I'm taking you around the city and giving you some of the history, the dark history of this place. And here we are, first stop. OK, you're looking at the site of one of the most famous Chicago legends.
T1 But… but these are just new apartment buildings.
G Er, yeah, that's right. But right here, on this spot, was the famous Lexington Hotel.
T1 A hotel? But I thought this was a crime tour?
G That's right, er… it is. OK, let me ask you. Do you know who lived at the Lexington Hotel? Al Capone. That's right! Mr Crime himself.
T2 Oh yeah! I've heard about him. And you're telling me he lived in a hotel? A major criminal…
G Well, he had to live somewhere, right? But this wasn't just any hotel. He had secret rooms in there and escape tunnels. He was prepared.
T1 So why didn't the police just go and get him?
G Oh, they tried. I mean, they wanted him for murder, for illegal alcohol, for corruption. He paid all the politicians, you know. And…
T2 So the politicians were protecting him?
G Well… Not all of them. The president, Herbert Hoover, personally asked for Capone's arrest in 1929. The police finally arrested him in 1931. And do you know what for? It wasn't because he had killed somebody, or for bribery or because he had robbed a bank or something. No, they arrested him because he hadn't paid tax for many years on his illegal money!

9.9

M = man   W = woman

M Did you hear about the teenager that was sent to jail for piracy? Peter Jackson, that's his name, I think.
W Oh, yeah? Like what, selling or just downloading stuff for personal use?
M Well, it says here that they found tens of thousands of mostly illegal movies and songs and games on his hard disk—more than 30 GB apparently.
W Whoa! That's a lot, isn't it?
M Oh, yeah. He'll appear in court next Tuesday, and he could get up to five years.
W What? For downloading stuff? That's not fair!
M Well, but it's more than that. Apparently, he had access to an advance copy of Transformers 4…
W You mean the DVD?
M The Blu-ray, I think. Anyway, so he made hundreds of copies… And started advertising them on Facebook before the movie was commercially available. It looks like he made a small fortune and…
W Oh, boy.
M So the studio took him to court and he was charged with…

9.10

W = woman   M = man

W But, honestly, do you? Do you think that's fair?
M What?
W A five-year sentence.
M Well, no, but I think he's got to spend some time in prison—at least a year, maybe. Otherwise, how else is he going to learn?
W Really? Come on. That is so unfair.
M What do you mean? I mean, I'm not saying he should be sentenced to life or anything, but…
W But he's young and he has his whole life ahead of him. And do we really want to put a boy like Peter in the middle of other dangerous criminals? I mean…
M So what exactly are you suggesting? That he should simply be acquitted? Just like that?
W No, of course not. Maybe he should, I don't know, pay a fine—I mean, a huge one—and then do some sort of community service or something. But definitely not go to jail.

Unit 10

10.1

M = man   W = woman

1 M1 Oh, I just can't stand days like this! Can you?
M2 What? You mean the meeting?
M1 Well, yeah, that was a pretty long one, but no. I mean this. All this rain, the grey skies, the cold… Winter just really depresses me. I can't wait for spring.
M2 Yeah, but it's good for the garden. And it cleans the city a little.
M1 Yeah, right.
M2 Oh, come on, it's not that bad. I mean, when it's like this you can't go out anyway, so it's better to be here at work. I mean, think about it. What else could you be doing?
M1 Yeah, I guess you've got a point. But still, I wish it would stop raining.

2 W Hey, look! This is where I went to school.
M Oh, what? That build… Hey! Look out!
W Oh! Idiot! Put your lights on! Idiot!
M Whoa! That was close.
W What an idiot! How am I supposed to see him at night if he doesn't put his lights on? Grrrr!
M I know. I hate it when people do that. It's so dangerous. The other day I was driving to…

3 M OK, that's five dollars and 78 cents. Is that everything?
W1 Er, yes… Yes, thank you. Er… Here, six.
M That's great. And 22 for you. Have a nice day!
W1 Thank you… Oh, that does annoy me!
W2 Er… What does?
W1 That! '22 for you! Have a nice day!' What is that about? Really, it's just so… So fake! I mean, I only want to buy some vegetables and some milk, it's not like we're best friends or anything. I mean, I don't know him, he doesn't know me… It's just, grrr!
W2 OK. I think you need to calm down a little. He's just doing his job.
W1 Ugh, really? It's just too much, it's so… plastic! Yuk! It's like, imagine if I meet a complete stranger and say…

10.3

J = John   B = Bob

1 J Hey, Bob. How's your new house project going?
B Oh! Hi, John. Well, we've put the walls up, as you can see. And the windows are coming next week, but it will be a while before we're living in it. But you know, we're getting there [beep].

R = radio   W = woman

2 R … and it looks like there's heavy traffic again on the major routes around the city, no surprises there. On the ring road there are…
W Heavy traffic, huh? Don't need to tell me! Oh, this traffic is driving me mad! I'm [beep].

M = man   S = Stewie

3 M Hey. What's up, Stewie? You look pretty down.
S Oh, you know… It's, well, it's Harriet.
M Oh, I see. So… Are you guys arguing again?
S Yeah, kind of.
M Look man, every relationship has [beep].

M = mother   J = Joel

4 M Joel! Joel… Have you tidied your room yet? Joel! I'm not going to tell you again. Go tidy your room before Granny gets here.
J Mum! I was playing. I almost beat him that time!
M Joel, I don't want to hear it. Now, get into your room and don't come out until it's tidy. I've told you [beep].

M = mother   S = son

5 M Ah. It's so good to finally have some [beep].
S Mum! Can I go home and play video games now?
M Ah…

10.6

1 You should apologise for saying that.
2 But who's responsible for solving those things?
3 I'm sick and tired of hearing that.
4 She does have a reason for complaining.
5 There are many ways of improving the city.

Answer Key

Unit 1

1.1
1 a 3 b 2 c 1 d 1 e 2 f 3 g 2
2 a What do you look for when you date someone? / When you date someone, what do you look for?
  b What were your teachers like last year?
  c What are you really good at?
  d If you could do something awesome right now, what would it be?
  e What's something you just can't live without?
  f Who would you like to go out with?
  g Which family members do you feel closer to?
3 g (baby) f (gorgeous) e (absolutely)
  d (really) c (either) a (well) b (anyway)
4 Personal answers.

1.2
1 Love Story 1: in, get, apart
  Love Story 2: on, for, They got, got
  Love Story 3: out, for, in, on, up, back
2 a 2 b 3 c 1
3 (8) Romeo dies, (6) escape, (1) meet, (9) Juliet dies, (7) get married secretly, (4) find out their families are enemies, (3) fall for each other, (2) get along well, (5) realize their love is impossible
4 Personal answers.
6 a They meet at a party and get on well immediately.
  b Their love is impossible but also irresistible.
  c The friar marries them secretly.
  d ... but they can't stay together.

1.3
1 a people you can count on.
  b people you are usually in contact with.
  c people you hang out with and get on well with. / people you get on well with and hang out with.
  d the people you can always rely on.
2 International UnFriend Day is a day for removing unnecessary people from Facebook.
3 helps you move house / has seen you recently
4 on, out, on, from, about, with
5 a acquaintances
  b very close friends
  c very close friends
  d acquaintances
  e friends
  f friends
6 Personal answers.
7 a Y b N c N d Y e N f Y g Y h N
  She should try a little harder.
8 a PS b PS c PP d PC e PS f PS g PP h PC

1.4
1 adventure-seeking, Outgoing, open-minded, like-minded, Easygoing, thoughtful
2 (text clues)
  in search of adventure
  funny, friendly, sociable
  isn't afraid of new ideas
  who enjoys nightlife and travel as much as I do
  with no worries
  Shy
3 do like / sure looks / really do love / sure am / do enjoy / am definitely

5 c, e, b, a, d

1.5
1 a Friendship b Love c Love d Friendship
  e Nothing f Nothing g Love
  h Friendship i Nothing j Nothing
2 b ADV c ADJ d N e V f N g N h V
3 1 Antony cheats on his wife, Fulvia.
  2 Fulvia dies and Antony goes back to Rome.
  3 Antony marries Caesar's sister, Octavia.
  4 Antony goes back to Egypt and Cleopatra.
  5 Caesar and Antony fight to control Egypt.
  6 Antony and Cleopatra both die.
5 WB: Song line 1.5: First dates.
  SB: Song line 1.1: Introductions.
  Song line 1.2: Falling in love.
  Song line 1.3: Photos of friends.
  Song line 1.4: Meeting people.

Unit 2

2.1
1 Not use regular electricity.
2 a F b F c T d F e F f T
3 a G (cups in this) b NG (for a couple)
  c NG (Can I have) d G (simple to be)
  e NG (Forget it) f NG (take a lift)
  g G (in the same)
4 b, a, d, e, g, f, c
5 b Do you buy any used clothes?
  c Do you have energy-efficient light bulbs at home?
  d Have you walked or cycled to work lately instead of using private transport?
  e Do you switch off appliances when you're not using them?
  f Do you use eco-friendly cleaning products?
  g Have you changed from plastic to reusable cloth bags?
6 c (John, gone, dog, stopped) d (top, lot, got, shop) a (hotel, road, open, phone)
  b (Don't, go, own, coat)

2.2
1 I haven't been taking taxis / I've been separating the rubbish / I haven't been buying disposable products / I've been buying more eco-friendly products
2 a Proud.
  b Wind and rain.
  c He is saving money.
  d No.
  e Yes.
  f Personal answer.
3 b Iceland
  c Switzerland
  d Costa Rica
  e Sweden
  f Norway
  g Brazil
  h France
4 a The office has been really busy. We've been working like mad.
  b I like your shoes. I've been trying to find a pair like that since last year.
    OR I was trying to find a pair like that last year.
  c So sorry! Have you been waiting for long?
  d Hey! I've been trying to phone you since yesterday. Where were you?
    OR I was trying to phone you yesterday.

  e He's been studying English for years.
    OR ... English for a year.
  f They've been playing football.
    OR They were playing football before.
  g Joan's been managing the advertising company since 2012.

2.3
1 a POACHING
  b DROUGHTS
  c FLOODS
  d DEFORESTATION
  e RISING SEA LEVELS
  f DUMPING OF E-WASTE
  g THREATENED SPECIES
  h FOSSIL FUELS
  i GLOBAL WARMING
2 Floods, droughts, deforestation, global warming.
3 a Floods.
  b No.
  c No.
  d 3 or 4 months ago.
  e 80%.
  f Israel.
4 a have replaced b have eliminated / have been planting / has planted c has developed / has dropped d have stopped / have become e have been trying
5 a How long have you known your best friend? (Since I was 11.)
  b Have you been working hard recently? (Yes, I have.)
  c Have you ever lived in a different city? (No, I haven't.)
  d How long have you been studying today? (For about 15 minutes.)
  e How much bread have you eaten today? (Not a lot.)
  f How far have you walked today? (Not far. About half a mile.)
  g How many cups of coffee have you drunk today? (Just a couple.)
  h Have you been exercising a lot lately? (Yes, I've been running and working out regularly.)

2.4
1 a 3 or 4
  b 5
  c 3
  d 1
  e 2
2 Tired of adverts? Try football streaming. 100% free. Only at livesport.com. High quality viewing.
  Want to find a new job? We can help you find the best job to match your strengths. Ring Work247. Speak to a job expert on 01632 960547
  Looking for your next professional challenge? Grabowsky & Loewe. Career Management. Contact us for a confidential discussion. www.G&Lcarreermanagement.com... or phone us on 01632 960979
  Laptop running slowly? Clean up tonnes of junk with TopClean, 3 in 1. One click cleaner frees up disk space. Security + eliminates harmful files. Performance automatically improves system preferences. Top Clean 3.1 for Mac or Microsoft
  Ready for professional growth? Congratulations! You've won a free online Chinese course. Learn the language that will open doors for intelligent shop assistants like you. Click here for a free introductory lesson.

3 a **Are you** ready for professional growth?
  b **Is your** laptop running slowly?
  c **Are you** looking for **your** next professional challenge?
  d **Do you** want to find a new job?
  e **Are you** tired of adverts?
4 a M b J c J d C e M f C
5 a came
  b 's been / haven't heard
  c 've reached
  d 've been working
  e ordered / hasn't arrived
  f checked / paid / 've been waiting

2.5

1 1 Javanese rhino 2 Golden lion tamarin
   3 Giant panda 4 Northern right whale
2 a I'm going to take a photograph.
  b I can see that they are eating fruit.
  c Hello and welcome to Zoo Atlanta.
  d Mother and child travelling along.
3 a Have you ever seen an endangered animal in the wild? / ~~a~~
  b Have you ever seen one in a zoo? / ~~a~~
  c Have you ever looked after a sick animal? / ~~on~~
  d Have you ever given money for an animal cause? / ~~never~~
  e Have you ever considered working for an animal protection NGO? / ~~it~~
4 20%, 33%, nearly 0%
5 a E
  b D
  c E
  d E
  e D
6 Person 1 wants to get a new job (phrase a).
  Person 2 wants to take a gap year (phrase e).
7 WB: Song line 2.5: Endangered animals / jungle.
  SB: Song line 2.1: Save the world / environment.
  Song line 2.2: Present perfect continuous.
  Song line 2.3: Present perfect simple and continuous.
  Song line 2.4: Present perfect simple and continuous

Unit 3

3.1

1 Across   Down
   1 smog   1 Statue
   2 Harbour   3 parks
   6 skyline   4 Bridge
   7 museums   5 slums
   8 skyscraper   6 square
2 a How do you like your city?
    a / the / the / the
  b Is it easy to find your way around?
    the
  c What's your favourite landmark?
    a / the
  d What are the most popular tourist spots?
    the
  They are talking about New York City.
3 Personal answers.
4 a Such a   c such   e Such
  b such   d Such an

3.2

1 a T b F c T d N e T f T
2 a had told b had sent c had made

  d had kissed e hadn't hugged
  f had mistaken g had shaken h had broken
3 a Did you know the Romans **spoke** Latin?
  b After we **arrived** home, we made some sandwiches.
  c By the time we got home, the TV show **had** finished.
  d When I had **had** lunch, I had a short nap.
  e We **bought** our car five years ago.
4 a gone   c been
  b been   d been
5 a Hi, this is your travel host, Naomi.
  b I'd like to show you the top ten attractions of Madrid, Spain.
  c Number ten. Plaza de Cibeles. Madrid is known for many beautiful squares like this one.
  d The Cibeles fountain is an important symbol of this city.
  e Number nine. Almudena Cathedral. It took more than a hundred years to complete its construction in 1993.
  f The original site was occupied by Madrid's first mosque.

3.3

1 'd been, 'd never been, chose, 'd read, grew up, couldn't, 'd never heard, took, helped, 'd imagined, would love; Liverpool.
2 To return to your story: 3, 4
  To check your listener understands what you mean: 1, 2
3 a H b N c H d H e H f L g N h L i N
4 a though b although c though d although
  e Even though
5 Personal answers.

3.4

1 a to a pop concert
  b to the theatre
  c out to eat
  d to the cinema
  e to a football match
2 c, a, f, b, d, g, e
3 a had been doing exercise
  b had been dancing
  c had been flying
  d had been fighting
  e had been speeding
4 a had been hanging out
  b had made / had been making
  c had got
  d had been dating
  e had killed
5 a I had to sit down because I'd been standing all day.
  b We got lost because we hadn't understood the directions.
  c OK
  d Vera had visited Turkey before so she knew the best places.
  e Until yesterday night, I had never had wine before.
  f OK
  g How long had you been waiting when the doors opened?

3.5

1 No cameras in the building.
2 a STOP IN THE NAME OF LOVE.
  b RESTRICTED AREA PRIVATE PROPERTY.
  c DO NOT ENTER, DIVE OR JUMP.

  d DO NOT TALK TOO MUCH. LET HER DRIVE.
  a and d are meant to be funny. Are they?
3 a Danger! No lifeguard **on** duty.
  b Kindly refrain **from** smoking.
  c Park here **at** your own risk.
  d Please clean **up** after your pet.
  e Tow **away** zone. Do not stop here.
  f Vehicles will be towed **at** owner's expense.
5 f, c, e, a, d, b
6 WB: 3.5 Song line: Signs.
  SB: Song line 3.1: Cities.
  Song line 3.2: Past perfect.
  Song line 3.3: Urban stress / City problems.
  Song line 3.4: Miss a chance.

Unit 4

4.1

1 literature, art, geography, maths, history, languages, chemistry, physics, biology
2 a R b D c R d R e D f D g R
3

Agree	Disagree
e	b, c
g	a
d	f

5 Do: badly, an exercise, homework, well
  Get: feedback, good marks, into trouble, kicked out, a report
  Make: a difference, mistakes, progress
  Take: an examination, photos, a test
6 d, c, f, g, a, b, e

4.2

1 b too much c too many d never enough
  e too much f too much g too little
  h no / too many i too much
2 a rich
  b problems
  c noise
3 d, b, e, f, a, c
5 food, future, much
7 walking to school / windy / Thursday / a café

4.3

1 b UK (US = dialogues)
  c US (UK = favourite)
  d US (UK = theatre)
  e UK (US = center)
  f US (UK = favour)
2 US = an apartment, a movie, a movie theater, a college student, a store, the drugstore, gas, a parking lot.
  UK = a flat, a film, a cinema, a university student, a shop, the chemist's, petrol, a car park.
3 b ... worked harder.
  c ... chosen art.
  d ... have dressed appropriately for the interview.
  e ... gone to music school when I had the chance.
  f ... have dropped out of uni.
5 a 2, 3, 5, 4, 1
  b 3, 2, 5, 1, 4
  c 4, 5, 1, 3, 2

4.4

1 c, e, f, a, d, b
2 a wouldn't have had to

b would have woken up
c had got
d had arrived
e would have understood
f would have passed
g wouldn't have got

3 b push
c shoe
d would
e put
f pull
g new

4 /uː/ shoe, blue, two, true, through, moved, moon, school, pool, new
/ʊ/ book, could, push, should, would, put, pull, cook, woman

5 b, d, a, —, c
Personal answers.

4.5

1 1 a, an, the, an, The
   2 the, a, a, a, the, a
   3 a, a, a, a, the, a

2 a Eight.
  b Ben Stiller is the only one who doesn't direct one of the three reviewed films. Jodie Foster is the only one who does two jobs in the same reviewed film.
  c *Little Man Tate* and *The Royal Tenenbaums*.
  d Jodie Foster.
  e *The Royal Tenenbaums*.
  f Jodie Foster.

3 a What's done is done. (S)
  b What were you thinking? (C)
  c It's not the end of the world. (S)
  d You should've known better. (C)
  e How could you do such a thing? (C)
  f Don't let it get you down. (S)
  g Will you ever learn? (C)

5 b You should've revised for the test.
    If you'd revised for the test, you wouldn't have failed.
  c You shouldn't have been absent a lot.
    If you hadn't been absent a lot, you wouldn't have got bad marks.
  d You shouldn't have cheated in the exam.
    If you hadn't cheated in the exam, you wouldn't have been kicked out of school.
  e You should've got into law school.
    If you'd got into law school, your parents wouldn't have been upset.

6 WB: Song line 4.5: The expression 'It's not the end of the world'.
  SB: Song line 4.1: Education.
  Song line 4.2: Making big changes.
  Song line 4.3: *Should have* + past participle.
  Song line 4.4: Third conditional.

Unit 5

5.1

1 1 g 2 c 3 e 4 b 5 h 6 f (*a*, *d* and *i* are not used.)

2 purchases, tags, save, statement, instalments, afford, spree, bargains, window, shopaholics

3 If you or someone close to you has a problem with compulsive shopping and spending, these tips can help.
  If you love-love-love to shop, ask yourself: Why?
  … if your spending is getting out of control, it's important to find out why.
  If your spending habits are affecting your life, stop buying in monthly instalments.
  If none of this works, and your spending is really out of control, look for counselling or therapy.

4 [word search grid]

5 a sunglasses, jeans, trousers, sandals, shorts, earrings, shoes
  b sunglasses, jeans, trousers, sandals, shorts, earrings, shoes, jewellery
  c scarf, bikini, hat, jacket, T-shirt, suit, bag

6 See audio script 5.1.

7 a isn't
  b isn't
  c is
  d Personal answer.
  e Personal answer.
  f Personal answer.

5.2

1 b, c, a, f, e, d

2 Net salary: £500
  Weekly [X]
  Amount applied for: £3,000
  Amount recommended: £2,000
  Interest rate: 8%
  First payment date: 1st July.
  Parent [X]

3 a has just
  b I only
  c agree to be
  d it's the
  e Depends
  f Will you

5

Silent *b*	Silent *t*	Silent *gh*	*gh* = /f/
doubt	fasten	bought	enough
thumb	listen	though	laugh

6 a bought
  b Fasten
  c thumb
  d listen / laugh
  e doubt / enough / though

5.3

1 a your clothes / your money / your name
  b your money / your chair / your word
  c your hair / a hairdryer / a towel
  d the letter *e* / the letter *s* / the letter *m*
  e food / poison / nothing

2 1 d   2 c   3 e

3 c, d, a, f, b, e

4 You must: be insane, be joking, be out of your mind
  You can't: seriously expect me / us to believe that

5 can't be serious, must be joking, must be insane, must be out of your mind, can't seriously expect me to believe that

5.4

1 a, c, b, d

2 Only the Hollywood sign.

3

Nouns		Verbs	
security	transaction	notify	
opportunity	auction	certify	

Adjectives		Adverbs	
ambitious	unbelievable	completely	
ridiculous	impossible	luckily	

4 a secure
  b marvellous
  c disappointment
  d washable
  e nicely
  f purify

5 1 a revolutionary electronic device
   2 the amazing ultra-absorbent towel
   3 OK
   4 This innovative air-conditioned shirt
   5 The fantastic wireless earpiece

5.5

1 c

2 a don't like
  b quick and quiet
  c similar to
  d Not getting lost
  e don't feel
  f seem to

3 c / C, b / C, a / SA, f / C, d / SA, e / C

4 Cash, Enter, declined, PIN, last

5 See audio script 5.12.

6 WB: Song line 5.5: Shopping.
  SB: Song line 5.1: Shopping.
  Song line 5.2: Losing your job.
  Song line 5.3: Modals of possiblity.
  Song line 5.4: Adverts.

Unit 6

6.1

1. What Makes Today's Serials More Addictive Than Ever Before?

2. a have / using b having c has d are e told
   Correct sequence according to paragraphs of the text: c, e, d, b, a.

3. a to (T)
   b of (F)
   c than (T)
   d for (F)
   e on (F)

4. a live sport
   b medical drama
   c the news
   d reality TV
   e soap operas
   f social media
   g chat show
   h websites

5. nouns: reality, soap, web; adjectives: live, medical, social; verb: chat; article: the

6. 1 c / h 2 e / a 3 d 4 b 5 g

6.2

1. a The / in / of (F)
   b The / of (T)
   c The / of (F)
   d of (F)
   e the / on (F)
   f of / the / on (F)

2. a The contestant **who is** leaving the island this week is Fifi. / *Survivor*.
   b The women who **live** in the house want to get married. / *The Bachelor*.
   c The island **that** we chose is very beautiful. / *Survivor*.
   d Kelly Osbourne recorded 'Papa Don't Preach' a song **that was** originally performed by Madonna. / *The Osbournes*.

3. a Nicki Minaj and Mariah Carey are the judges whose fights on camera were popular on Twitter.
   b Catherine is the girl who / that won the diamond engagement ring.
   c The location that the organisers choose is usually far away from civilisation.
   d Ozzy is a famous heavy metal vocalist whose family appeared on MTV.
   e Kim's the woman who / that won after the other 14 contestants left the island.
   f He's chosen a song that is close to his heart.
   g The dances that the professionals teach can be difficult.

4. 1 that
   2 who
   5 that
   7 that

5. a turned up b turns out c turns into
   d took turns

6.3

1. d, a, b, X, f, c, e

2. ..., **who** is the latest Mr Bond, / ..., **whose** single 'Skyfall' played all over the world for months, / **that** has reached every corner of the planet / ..., **who** created and directed most of the movies / ..., **whose** novels sold millions of copies to all age groups / ..., **which** were mainly written in a café, / **that** she created

3. **Spider-Man:** Spider-Man, who was originally a Marvel superhero, has had five films. (N) The fourth one premiered in 2012 with a cast that included a new Spider-Man played by Andrew Garfield. (R)
   Mary Jane Parker, who was the love interest between 2002 and 2007, was cut from the 2012 and 2014 films. (N)
   Twilight Saga: Author Stephanie Meyer, whose novels inspired five films so far, must be pretty pleased with the amazing success of her *Twilight* saga. (N)
   These vampire films, which have captivated teenagers worldwide, (N) tell of beautiful hair, perfect bodies, dreamy kisses and the violent battles that the Cullens and their wolf friends fight against the Volturi. (R)

4. a *The Dark Knight* / which is my favourite Batman movie / won four Oscars.
   b Heath Ledger / who played the scariest Joker ever seen / won an Academy Award after he died.
   c Christian Bale / who played Batman / wasn't nominated for an Oscar for his part.
   d This sentence doesn't have speech pauses, because it is a restrictive relative clause.
   e *Pirates of the Caribbean* / which was inspired by Disneyworld's attraction / has made over 5 billion dollars so far.

6.4

1. a Fame is **like** caviar, you know? It's good to have it, but not when you have it at every meal.
   b Wealth is **like** seawater; the more we drink, the thirstier we become; and the same is true of fame.
   c I just use my muscles **as** a conversation starter.
   d Fame, you know, it's **like** a hand gun—in the wrong hands, it's dangerous.
   e Don't quit! Suffer now and live the rest of your life **as** a champion.

2. a It's called work.
   b No, in any circumstances.
   c It can destroy your private life completely.
   d It's entertainment.
   e Theatres, clubs and cinemas.
   f At least five friends.
   g It means you're already infected and work already controls your life.

3. a Make sure you go home on time.
   b Think about having a holiday.
   c Always have enough water to drink.
   d Never try to do more than you can.
   e If you take regular breaks, you'll be more efficient.

4. 1 church / Katy Perry
   2 beauty / Rihanna
   3 McDonald's / Pink
   4 hotel porter / Tom Cruise
   5 tobacco cutter / George Clooney
   6 songwriter / Lady Gaga

5. start, win, earn, work, work, have

6.5

1. on, on, in, in, on, in, in, on, on

2. a for (F)
   b as (T)
   c of (T)
   d as (T)
   e like (T)

3. a

4. a baked
   b furnished / specific
   c pair / French lamps
   d photo of
   e short / eat
   f an Adele / you must

6. WB: Song line 6.5: Preposition 'like'.
   SB: Song line 6.1: TV / Radio programmes.
   Song line 6.2: Restrictive relative clause.
   Song line 6.3: Non-restrictive relative clause.
   Song line 6.4: Film words.

Unit 7

7.1

1. clutch, brake, bonnet, engine, steering wheel, accelerator, boot, tyres, wipers, windscreen.
   Car producers: Mercedes-Benz, Volkswagen

2. boot, clutch, wipers, bonnet, steering wheel

3. a accelerator / brake
   b windscreen
   c tyre
   d engine

4. a off
   b down
   c off
   d on
   e up
   f on
   d, f, b, a, e, c

5. b it down
   c turn them off
   d I'll put it on
   e OK, I'll turn it up.
   f OK, I'll turn them on.

7.2

1. tell, tell, say, say, tell, tell, say, say, say

2. a 2 b 5 c 3 d 1 e 4

3. 1 I was a great cook 2 I didn't look fat
   3 he liked romantic comedies 4 he didn't look at other women 5 he was sorry

4. a was
   b he would
   c we could
   d she looked
   e she hadn't married
   f had / him

5. Anna said / told Mark (that) she had never been interested in marriage.
   Mark said he knew (that) Anna loved him.
   Anna told Mark that she couldn't marry him.
   Anna told Mark she was in love with someone else.

7.3

1. b

2. a, b, c, e, g

3. a Can you tell me...
   b I wonder if...
   c I have no idea if...
   d I need to know if...
   e Do you know if...
   f Do you have any idea...
   g Could you tell me...

4. b you have installed iTunes on your computer

c I have no idea what you're talking about.
d I need to know if you're familiar with the different icons.
e Do you know if you have a Mac or a PC?
f Do you have any idea when you bought it?
g Could you tell me how I can upload music to my tablet?

5 b where I live.
c if I have a fast car.
d when I started learning English.
e if I can dance well.
f who I would take to a desert island.

6 /ʊ/ pull, push, put, cushion, notebook, full
/ʌ/ plug, button, cut, under, comfortable, shut, bug

7.4

1 b What did you do
c Do you like
d will you finish
e Are you
f has your / improved

2 a Sue asked me **not to** ring her tonight.
b I asked her where **she was** going.
c She asked me why **I wanted** to know.
d I told her **not to** be rude to me.
e She **told** me to leave her alone.

3 a Q b R c Q d Q e R f Q g Q h R
4 f, b, e, g, c, h, a
5 a F b T c T d T e F
6 Student: He told you to raise your arm.
Student: He asked you to stand up.
Student: He told you to take this medicine.

7.5

1 d, f, e, b, a, c
2 Personal answers.
3 e, a, c
(suggested answers)
b + ppl text than ring
d Libraries – customers now
f games + common smartphone use < 15 yrs

4 a What's your point
b that's exactly my point
c point taken
d you have a point
e get to the point

5 a It depends on what you mean by… / of
b Hold on a second, let me finish. / in
c We can't deny that… / to
d That may be true, but… / is
e I couldn't agree more. / be
f I totally disagree. / am

6 1 c   4 f
  2 a   5 d
  3 b   6 e

7 WB: Song line 7.5: Social networks.
SB: Song line 7.1: Car-related vocabulary.
Song line 7.2: Reported speech.
Song line 7.3: Indirect questions.
Song line 7.4: Reported speech.

Unit 8

8.1

1 The man.
2 1 tanning bed 2 laser hair removal
  3 moisturiser 4 hair gel 5 mascara
  6 lipstick

3 a himself b themselves c myself
  d herself e ourselves f itself

4 putting on, stick to, cut down, cut out, take up, work out

5 a F b T c T d F e T f T
Personal answer.

6 a look like b ✓ c ✓ d looks younger e ✓
f looks like

8.2

1 c, e, b, a, d
2 a must've come
b can't have been
c must've won
d might've overslept
e can't have seen

3 The father is criticising and the mother is sympathising. / Personal answer.

4 a doesn't like
b responsible
c didn't ask
d wouldn't
e not going

5 a he must've wanted
b can't have been last
c might have decided to do it
d must've saved up a lot of
e could've been a lot

8.3

1 2, 1, 3
2 a implant in her eye, but they didn't do it / she couldn't get it done there.
b a diamond put in her tooth.
c a tattoo, but then she broke up with Jason.
d wants to get the tattoo removed as soon as possible.

3 a D b F c D d F e F f T g T
5 Personal answers.
6 Personal answers.

8.4

1 Across
2 ceiling 5 pillow 6 sheet 7 wall 8 floor
Down
1 bedside table 3 lamp 4 blanket 9 rug

2 a More
b many
c are

3 bed, bed, ceiling, floor, desk, lamps, desk, desk, bed, floor

4 a are you ? ↘ b isn't it? ↘ c don't you? ↘
d didn't you? ↗ e will he / she? ↗ f won't you? ↗ g wouldn't you? ↘

8.5

1 a Open your ears
b More than the language
c Guessing is good
d Don't be afraid!

2 a Songs, streamed TV shows, podcasts.
b It's expensive and language classes don't always focus on listening.
c Learn about their culture.
d Learn to focus on the words you know and trust your guesses for the ones you don't.
e Everybody will be pleased that you are trying and the more you try, the better you'll feel.

3 a comfortable
b communication
c essential
d expensive
e insecurity
f obviously

4 both / … more important **than** reading and writing.
better / … and I want **to** improve.
either / … but I couldn't **understand** either of them.
to / They are **easier** to understand.
either / … do you think **so**?

5 WB: Song line 8.5: Listening.
SB: Song line 8.1: Appearance and vanity.
Song line 8.2: Modal perfects.
Song line 8.3: Causative form.
Song line 8.4: Question tags.

Unit 9

9.1

1 a a bribe
b to kidnap
c to go to prison
d to steal

2 1 5
2 6
3 4
4 3

3 1 Lots of locals told me to be extra careful.
2 Got stopped for speeding. Police officer didn't accept bribe. Stupid.
3 Theft is when someone takes something without you knowing.
4 OK, I think I can help you. Theft is when someone takes something from you.

4
Crime	Criminal	Verb
bribery		to bribe (sb)
burglary	a burglar	to break into (a house)
drug dealing	a drug dealer	to deal drugs
kidnapping	a kidnapper	to kidnap (sb)
murder	a murderer	to murder / kill (sb)
robbery	a robber	to rob (person / place)
theft	a thief	to steal (sth)

5 b Bribery
c have kidnapped
d organised crime
e robbery
f stole

6 a He's Al Capone.
b He lived in a hotel.
c The president of the USA at the time.
d He was arrested because he hadn't paid taxes for many years on his illegal money.

7 a are looking
b Do / know
c 've heard
d hadn't paid

9.2

1 a Medellín was recently named the world's most innovative city. / ~~of~~
b It was judged by eight different criteria. / ~~were~~
c Public spaces were created and government programmes reached these communities. / ~~was~~

d This neighbourhood was once considered a dangerous slum. / by

2 ⊕, ⊖, ⊕, ⊕, ⊖, ⊕

3 was, am, was, is, is, has been
'There is the place…' is not passive voice.

4 a 2 b 4 c 1

5 a An alternative system **was developed**. It's **considered** a success.
b Curitiba's bus system **is often compared** to an underground railway, Curitiba's buses **are used** by its 2.3 million residents.
c The BRT system **has been adopted** in / by 83 cities worldwide. **It will soon be implemented** by / in parts of Chicago.

9.3

1   2   1
    4   3
    5   6
    8   7
    10 9

2 Let it expire before you renew it., Try using your name and birthday—nobody will guess that!, Don't use the Internet at home.

3 a Hotspot / *hotspot*
b Track / *track* (any verb form)
c Up-to-date / *up-to-date*
d Target / *target*
e Password / *password*
f Click / *click*

4 a You can make your computer more secure **by** using virus protection software.
b The last guests had arrived **by** 10pm.
c The malware was uploaded **by** some hackers.
d I'll be home **by** midnight. I may get home before that.
e Tony improved a lot **by** working hard.

5 a F b F c T d T   Sam is man A.

6 a 'll be working
b wants it by
c I'll have
d will have been

7 a won't have / won't be having fun
b won't have finished the report by / won't finish the report on
c will see / is seeing / is going to see / will be seeing his children

9.4

1 NY teen arrested for selling movie before official release date

2 a F b F c T d T

3 be acquitted   (N)
do community service   (W)
pay a fine   (W)
be sentenced to life   (N)
be sentenced to one year in prison   (M)

4 1 c   2 a

5 a B b A c B d B e F f B

7 a under b on c on d for e of
Personal answers.

9.5

1 c

2 4, 5, 1, 3, 2

3 a, d, b

4 a F b T c F d F e F f F

5 a Where will you be living in five years' time?
b Are you good at making excuses?

c Have you ever been to court?
d Does crime often worry you?
e What was your best birthday present ever?
f How could your city be improved quickly?

6 WB: Song line 9.5: Giving excuses.
SB: Song line 9.1: Crime.
Song line 9.2: Passive voice.
Song line 9.3: Future continuous.
Song line 9.4: Punishment.

Unit 10

10.1

1 d, e, a, b, c
The Malcolm X quote sees anger as a positive emotion.

2 seldom, bring about, complaining

3 1 weather 2 bad drivers 3 insincerity

4 a T b F c T d F e F f F

6 a 3 b 1 c 2 d 5 e 4

10.2

1 1 Car modifications
2 Chewing gum
3 Eating on public transport

2 a 3 b 2 c 1 d 1 e 3

3 for making / Stopping / meeting / throwing / listening / of complaining

4 A, D, D, A, D, D

5 should apologise for saying that, responsible for solving those things, sick and tired of hearing, have a reason for complaining, There are many ways of

10.3

1 a for b of c about d about e of f for g about

2 a stopped to ask for directions / stopped asking for directions
b tried to open the door / tried opening the door
c remember to visit my grandparents / remember visiting your grandparents
d stopped to buy milk / stopping buying milk

3 being a kid, Knowing, saying, to think, taking, to yell, Learning

4 is played, works, explodes, is ordered, been humiliated, was trying

5 a Why don't we stop to have a break?
b I don't remember putting them there.
c Have you tried drinking some water?
d Could you please stop doing that!
e Please, try to remember.

10.4

1 a 7 b 16 c 6 d 7 e 4

2 a You meet each other's needs equally.
b We'll tell you how to get rid of a toxic friendship in four easy steps.
c Do they seem jealous of me?
d Don't be afraid of this person.
e Learn to love yourself.

3 myself, myself, myself, yourself, themselves, yourself, themselves

4 f, d, b, j, a, e, h, i, g, c

5 a Did you **grow up** in this city?
No, I moved here when I was 21.
b Have you got today's newspaper?
Oh, sorry, I **threw it away** after I read it.
c Have you uploaded your holiday photos yet?

No, I haven't **got around to it** yet. I'll do it tomorrow.
d You know, biting your fingernails is a really bad habit.
Yeah, I know. I should try to **give it up**.
e Er, Jim? I've got a little problem with the police.
Well, don't come to me! You **got into it**, you can get yourself out of it!
f Have we got any orange juice left in the fridge?
No, we **ran out of it** last night.
g Hank hasn't returned any of my calls and…
Sue, you need to **wise up**. Seriously, that guy is bad news.
h That sounds like a bad cough. Did you see a doctor already?
No, not yet. I guess I shouldn't **put it off** any longer. I'll make an appointment tomorrow.
i So lunch was… a bottle of cola, a doughnut and…
Wait! I've heard enough. Seriously, if you continue to eat like that you'll **end up** losing your teeth, or worse.
j Do you know Clara?
Of course I do. We **get on** great. We've known each other for years.

10.5

1 c, d, a, f, b, e

2 a I told **her** it **was** difficult and asked her to help me.
b A lot of new hotels are **being built** in my city.
c OK.
d My dad complains **about getting** up early in the morning.
e I can't remember where **my car is**.
f OK.
g OK.
h How long **have you been living in** this city?
i OK.
j She works **as** a secretary for a company **that** specialises in import / export.

3 1 find / to read
2 at remembering
3 difficulty
4 Listening
5 It's

4 1 d You should **consider reading** things you're interested in.
2 e Have you **thought** about **keeping** a notebook for new words?
3 a A good way of **improving** your pronunciation **is recording** yourself.
4 b Try **to focus** on the stressed words.
5 c How about **learning** some common phrases like 'I mean' or 'you know'?

5 Personal answers.

6 WB: Song line 10.5: Mistakes.
SB: Song line 10.1: Moody people.
Song line 10.2: Therapy.
Song line 10.3: Gerund.
Song line 10.4: Phrasal verbs.

Phrase Bank

This Phrase Bank is organised by topics.
▶ The audio is on the ID portal, unit by unit.

Getting to know people

Unit 1
Have you got any nicknames?
Are you usually more optimistic or pessimistic?
What's the first thing you notice when meeting someone new?
Where do you and your family come from?
What did you want to be when you were young?
Which football team do you and your family support?

Expressions when you need extra time

Unit 1
Well, let's see…
Hmm, let me think…
Er, I'm not sure. I'd have to think about that…
That's a difficult one. Er…
That's a good question. Well…
Er, it depends on the context.

Relationships

Unit 1
I've met them, but I don't know everyone well.
Hmm. They have a lot in common, but I still think their personalities are too different.
My sister broke up with her boyfriend last year, but they got back together after a week.
Oh yeah? Are they still together?
I'd definitely go for shared interests. It's important to have fun together.
My father met my mother when she crashed into his car one day.
It depends if you're talking about people you met once or twice or real friends you know well.
We've known each other since school. We used to be really close.

Talking about online dating

Unit 1
It's for losers who have been dumped. Period.
It's pretty useless if you want to build a solid relationship.
I think it's easier to find love online than in real life.
It helps people focus on personality rather than looks.
I'd try if I was really desperate.

Asking for and giving opinions

Unit 1
I do believe that…
People do seem to…
I do agree that…
I definitely think that…

Unit 2
I'd never try the green diet 'cause I don't like vegetables, you know, rabbit food.
Hmm… maybe I'd go to the retreat. I need a rest.

Unit 3
Our city has a lot of problems. I love it, though.
Really? I don't. I'm tired of living here.
How do you feel about…?
What do you think of…?

Unit 4
And I think uniforms are a good idea. It's one less decision to make in the morning.
No way! I love wearing my own clothes.

Unit 5
Life's too short. What's the point of saving too much money?
Men often buy things they can't afford just to impress their friends.
It's better to shop online than spend hours at the shop.
That is so sexist!
I see what you mean, but I think it's partly true.

Reactions

Unit 1
I'm surprised.
No way!
Is this true?
Are you serious?
Hang on a sec.
You mean the date?
So what happens next?
And then?
Oh, dear.

Unit 3
Oh yeah? How come?
No way! I do that all the time!
Who do you think you are to talk to me like that?
What do you mean?
You poor thing!
You're joking! Gee! And how did it turn out?
No wonder!
Well, I'm sure something better will come along…
What do you mean I can't park here? Says who?
Oh, come on! Be reasonable!

Unit 4
Really? What did you do?
Why would you say such a thing?

Unit 5
No way! You must be joking!
Are you insane? You can't be serious!

Going green

Unit 2
Do you have water-efficient taps in your home?
On our own, none of us can really make much difference.
Yeah, but every little thing helps.

Talking about duration

Unit 2
He's been driving a brand new car since Monday.
She used to watch a lot of TV, but she's been watching far less TV since she saw the film.
Really? How long have you been going there?
How long have you been reading it?
Yeah, the battery has died twice, but only because he's been using Twitter a lot.
No way! How long have you been collecting iPods?

Unit 3
Yeah, and he had been trying to find a job for a long time.
We'd been away for two weeks, so…

The environment

Unit 2
I don't believe that only humans cause global warming.
There's no consensus that global warming exists.
Animals and plants can adapt to global warming.
It's the sun that's getting warmer.
Temperatures haven't increased since 1998, so what's the big deal?
We have had ice ages and warmer periods. Climate change is natural.
What do you mean global warming? It's freaking cold!
Floods are a real problem in São Paulo.
And it's got worse recently.

Describing places

Unit 3
That's the fashionable neighbourhood.
OK, it's next to the sea and there are some small islands.
Well, my cousin went there and she had such a good time. Also, it has really beautiful beaches.
Last year I went to this amazing place, you know. I'd never been there before and…
I loved most of the landmarks. I thought Big Ben was amazing.
At first I hated the food, but by the time I left I'd got used to it.
I was shocked to find out how fast Londoners spoke.
I thought some neighbourhoods were kind of poor and scary at night.

Urban problems

Unit 3
I think the worst problem by far is all the thieves.
No way! The potholes are much more annoying.
I love this city, but New Yorkers don't respect traffic signs!
Although I love this city, I can't stand the crime.
There's rubbish everywhere I go!
The noise drives me mad!
I can't stand people who go through red lights.
There are massive traffic jams in my city, but that doesn't bother me at all. I'm a cyclist!

Making guesses and deductions

Unit 3
I guess the first one could be outside a restaurant?
Yep, or maybe the entrance to a shop?

Unit 5
Maybe John Smith's a sick boy or something like that.
Yeah, makes sense. Or maybe…
I think he must be talking to his son.
Hmm… Not sure. I think he might be talking to a friend.
I think the first one might be true, but I'm not really sure.
Really? I actually think it could be bad for your teeth.
You look fit. I think you might work out a lot in your free time.
Yeah, I saw you carrying a tennis racket the other day. You must play tennis.
Hmmm. I'm not sure. It's hard to tell.
I'd say it's probably about consumer behaviour.

Reinforcing

Unit 3
I'm afraid so.
I'm afraid not.

Apologising

Unit 3
I'm sorry. I didn't realise that.
Whoops! Sorry again.

School life

Unit 4
Maybe they have a lot of expensive private schools.
Yes, or else education could all be completely free.
Students usually behave well there, but in my old school they didn't.
At my school, students get too much homework. It takes me four or five hours a day.
I think schools should make us feel special because we all learn in different ways.
You're right, but equal opportunity is essential.

Picking a career

Unit 4
I can't throw away £9,000, drop out of uni, forget about my business degree and start all over again.
I'd love to get a scholarship to go to law school, but it's so hard I won't even try.
All my friends will do a summer placement, so that's what I'll do.
My parents have always wanted me to get into medical school. I can't disappoint them, and they are desperate for me to succeed.
I'd love to get a degree in music, but what will I do when I graduate? How will I get a decent job?

I have all the education I need; I'm not illiterate! It's time for fun, fun, fun!
I'd study gastronomy at the Sorbonne.
Yep, me! I tried three completely different jobs until I found the right one for me.

Regrets

Unit 4

I should've chosen another course.
I should've thought about it more carefully.
Should I have persevered a little more?
I shouldn't have listened to him.
I shouldn't have missed so many lessons.
Me too. I should have studied harder.
I should've checked my new messages.

Hypothetical situations in the past

Unit 4

I would've paid that bill if I'd had time. I swear.
If I'd tidied up my office, I wouldn't have lost that report.
Well, you wouldn't have failed physics if you'd done your homework, that's for sure.
Look, I would've done the washing up if you'd asked me to. If you hadn't spent the whole night partying, you wouldn't have overslept… and we wouldn't be in trouble now.

Criticising

Unit 4

Will you ever learn?
You should've known better.
How could you do such a thing?
What were you thinking?

Expressing sympathy

Unit 4

It could've been worse.
Don't let it get you down.
What's done is done.
It's not the end of the world.

Shopping

Unit 5

Do you ever pay in monthly instalments?
Er… only for really expensive things, like my motorbike.
When I go window shopping, I end up spending money I hadn't planned to.
I can't resist a bargain. When I see 'reduced' on a price tag, I buy it even if I don't really need it.
I'm afraid to check my credit card statement at the end of the month.
I'd rather buy something nice than save money for future emergencies.
I pay for a lot of things in monthly instalments.
Whenever I overspend, I hide purchases from friends and family.
I borrow money from friends and relatives to buy things I can't afford.
I go on shopping sprees with my friends for fun or on my own when I'm anxious or depressed.

Talking about products

Unit 5

I bought some really expensive sunglasses and left them in a taxi. I felt really guilty afterwards.
I bought it on impulse. It was pure madness!
It seemed like a wonderful product, but it was such a disappointment.
The thing was actually very dangerous.
It could have hospitalised you, but not really killed you. Come on!
There was no technical assistance at all.
It was fashionable at the time, I guess.

Shopping problems

Unit 5

I like these shoes. Can I try them on?
What size do you wear?
Have you got a size ten in stock?
I'm sorry madam, we're sold out.
Typical! Why do you never have larger sizes? I'm not coming here again!
Cash or charge?
Swipe your card, please.
Ah. I'm afraid your card has been declined.
Declined! But that's ridiculous! It's a new card, and I know I'm not over my limit. Your machine must be broken.
I'd like to return this TV. I bought it here the other day and it doesn't work.
Well, er, unfortunately we can't give you a refund, but we'd be happy to exchange it for another one.
Sure, er, I just need to see your receipt.

Other useful expressions

Unit 1

I guess one advantage is that you meet a lot of different people.

Unit 2

I need a lot of encouragement to get out of bed on Mondays.

Unit 3

My first car ride wasn't too bad. I'd never driven on the left side of the road.
You should be careful and only take official taxis.

Unit 4

I always put off doing the washing up, especially on weekends. What about you?

Unit 5

Supermarket psychology doesn't work on me 'cause I only buy the basics.

TV

Unit 6
I don't watch a lot of TV, but I sometimes watch…
That's not me at all. I'm really into…
I often watch TV on my tablet in bed, especially in winter.
The first TV I remember was in black and white, and it was massive.
When I was a kid, we watched TV together in the evening as a family.

Describing people

Unit 6
She's a singer that I really don't care about.
He's an American TV presenter who interviews famous people.
… who / which I'm really into…
… which very few people know…
… who's one of the best in the world…
… whose songs are downloaded in millions…

Giving opinions

Unit 6
I'm kind of curious about…
I heard a great song on YouTube last week. It was by…
Oh, I've seen that video. I didn't like it, to be honest.
Twitter is the best place to talk about TV now.

Unit 7
I think they're becoming less and less interested in foreign affairs.
I'd never read that book. I mean, life's too short.
Don't trust anyone under 30? Come on!
I think the weakest arguments are the ones about his son. I mean, who cares?
Computers will soon replace teachers.
People should learn Chinese instead of English.
The Internet needs to be more strongly regulated.
People who don't recycle their waste should be arrested.
Yeah, I couldn't agree more.
My point exactly!

Unit 9
I think all of them were pretty stupid, but the guy who showed his ID was the worst.
I really like the one about the importance of being proud of your city. I mean…
That's why I really think songs, books and music should be completely free.

Making deductions

Unit 6
He's saying something like 'Help! Don't hurt me!'
I think 'viewers' means people that…
I'm sure one of them must be *Iron Man 3*.

Unit 7
Maybe the director said…
The first one could be a shop assistant.
I think the first one could be a piano.
Maybe. Or a mobile phone. That would make sense.

Unit 8
I imagine the first one probably belongs to a single man because…

Unit 9
First one… Well, let's see. Maybe he left his driving licence at the shop and went back to get it?
Do you think these people are a gang or something?
I think the burglar is going to say he entered the wrong house.

Expressing surprise

Unit 6
What? Get out of here!
Really? You're joking, right?
No way! You mean your sister actually studied with Tom Cruise?
My goodness!
Are you serious?
That can't be true. I don't believe you.

Unit 7
Oh, yeah? How come?

Talking about technology

Unit 7
I hate it when they freeze while I'm working on something.
Same here. And those awful error messages!
I always leave my mobile phone on. I'm too lazy to turn it off.
Yeah, me too. Sometimes it's embarrassing when it rings.
No, I guess I'm just lucky when I buy things.
My sister's scared of machines, especially smartphones.
Oh, yeah? But she does have a smartphone, right?
I can't get this remote control to work.
Hi, I'm phoning about the chair. There are a few things I need to know.
Can you ask the car to turn on the engine?
My satnav is voice-activated, but it's kind of stupid.
I get annoyed when my satnav tries to be funny. Its jokes are terrible. I just want it to shut up and do its job.
Look, it has just arrived!
Oh, yes, you can mount it on the wall yourself.
It works just as well as the famous brand, but it's half the price.
You'll be able to use it in any country, don't worry.
Some of the keys are different, but it's basically the same thing.

Phrase Bank

Unit 9
I try to create really difficult passwords.

Indirect questions

Unit 7
I wonder if you can help me.
Do you remember when you bought it?
Do you know where it is?
Can you tell me what it says?

Reporting

Unit 7
This guy I met at a club told me he was single.
And you said he was smart.
He asked if he bored me.
I asked him if he was hungry.
I asked her to text someone.
I asked if the weather would get worse.
I asked him if he loved me.
I asked him to call me an ambulance.
I told him to make me a coffee.

Appearance

Unit 8
The wrinkles are almost gone!
Maybe Zoe had cosmetic surgery because of her husband.
Not exactly worry, but I'm careful about what I eat.
So, have you ever been overweight?
No idea at all. Maybe shampoo or something?
I think talent is as important as appearance for celebrities.
Well, those two look like friends, but…

Speculating about the past

Unit 8
That must've taken, like, ages!
The new look may have helped.
She might have thought we were making fun of her.
That can't have been easy.
What do you think happened in the first one?
The driver might have put it on his car or something. And you?

Unit 9
Hmm… I don't know. It might've been a mistake.

Actions / Services other people do for you

Unit 8
We still need to have the cake made.
We're going to have a new dress made.
I got my nails done too.
Dad still hasn't got it cleaned.
Did you have it straightened?
Really? I don't know how to. I'd have to get it fixed.

Really? I think he had it painted.
I can't stand the living room. I'm going to have it repainted one of these days.

Expressing preferences

Unit 8
I don't know. I kind of like it.
I prefer Ray-Ban. Their designs are cooler.
Which one are you better at, grammar or vocabulary?
Two people in my group prefer grammar to vocabulary.
Well, here everybody likes vocabulary better.

Unit 10
What a stupid quiz! I'm not like that at all!

Asking for confirmation

Unit 8
You really like baseball, don't you?
The new Myspace logo is weird, isn't it?
Barry painted the lamp, right?

Crime and punishment

Unit 9
To me, credit card fraud is the least serious crime.
Well, it depends on the amount of money you steal, doesn't it?
Most students – four out of five actually – think credit card fraud has increased.
Wasn't Mel Gibson arrested for drink-driving?
Yeah! And then he insulted the police and made it worse.
I think the old lady should be sentenced to at least ten years.
No, that's not fair. I mean, what if she dies in prison?

Talking about the future

Unit 9
We won't be driving electric cars any time soon.
By 2025, cyber attacks will have become the world's top threat.
Attacks will be carried out wirelessly, and we won't be protected.
Viruses will spread across multiple devices very, very easily.
Twenty percent of all world smartphones will have been targeted.

Giving excuses

Unit 9
I sometimes say I'm busy when I'm not.
Just a minute! This is not what it looks like. I was just…
Just hear me out!
It's not what you're thinking.
It's not what it seems.
Hold on! I can explain.

Moods

Unit 10
How often do you yell at people when you're angry?
Not me. I'm much more emotional than that.
I get really grumpy when I'm on a diet.
Me too. I start yelling at people for no reason. It's awful!
No, I don't have pet hates. I'm cool as a cucumber!
People who change the TV channel without asking. I hate that!
Yeah! And taxi drivers who know everything and talk too much!
I'm sick and tired of…

Learning English

Unit 10
Do you ever look up new words online?
All the time, but I do try to guess them first.
Let's see… First one… I agree. I think I'm good at grammar.
I'm not. I'm good at listening, but I'm really bad at grammar.
A lot of words change when they join together.
I have no trouble learning grammar – especially verb tenses. But I find pronunciation hard, like the *th* sound, for example.

Making recommendations

Unit 10
I love www.ted.com. Hundreds of different video talks to watch.
For me, the best advice for Bruna is the one thing she didn't say.
Have you thought about paying attention to the *th* sound in English films? It worked for me.

Other useful expressions

Unit 6
Well, I guess it's important to get permission to film in some places.
Yeah, and to choose the correct light too.
Did I ever tell you that my sister went to school with Tom Cruise?
Yeah. They went to school together.
Yep, and I think he asked her why she wears clothes like that.
Well, I'd like to ask her where she gets her inspiration from.
I recognised the singing; my cousin used to do the dance.

Unit 7
OK, so he said 'cat', but he meant 'car'. I guess 'blood' could be…
No, I don't think so – at least I've never seen anything like that.

Unit 8
There's a guy at work who is always talking about other people.
I'd probably fix a broken tap myself.
Mum, I need to talk to you about your phone.
What's the matter?
I like to have a meal with my family.
I was an only child, so yeah, my mum spoiled me a lot.

Unit 9
Well, he started listening to…
Hey, what do you think you're doing?

Unit 10
Taliesin, welcome to the group. What brings you here?
Yeah, I think so. A friend of mine took a course like this once.
In the first one, I'd probably stop going to those family meals.
Both. But they react differently.
So… Some relationships can take away our energy and…
One of my best friends used to bully me. It took me a long time to realise it. We don't speak anymore.

Word List

This is a reference list. To check pronunciation of any individual words, you can use a talking dictionary.

Unit 1

Relationships
to be attracted to someone
to be dumped
to break up
to drift apart
to fall out with someone
to get on (well)
to get (back) together
to get to know someone better
to have a crush on someone
to settle down

Personality adjectives
adventure-seeking
easygoing
financially stable
fun-loving
kind-hearted
knowledgeable
like-minded
nerdy
open-minded
outgoing
thoughtful

Other words
childless
inner beauty
long-lasting
shallow
suitable
take-out
uptown

Unit 2

Going green
appliances
bottled water
disposable products
eco-friendly
energy-efficient light bulb
fans
household waste
insecticides
nature-friendly
polystyrene cup
plastic bags
refillable bottles
renewable energy
reusable cloth bag
solar heating
stand-by mode
solar panel
tap

The environment
deforestation
droughts
dumping
floods
fossil fuels
global warming
ice ages
poaching
rising sea levels
threatened species

Threatened species
Giant panda
Golden lion tamarin
Hawaiian monk seal
Ivory-billed woodpecker
Javanese rhino
Mountain gorilla
Northern right whale

Other words
bird food
pull someone's heartstrings

Unit 3

Cities
harbour
landmark
neighbourhood
skyline
skyscraper
slum
smog
square

Adjectives
chaotic
exceptional
flat
magnificent
ugly
upmarket

Social conventions and manners
to blow your nose in public
to blow on your soup
to bow
to chew
to hug
to kiss on the cheek
to leave a tip
to push your way through the crowd
to shake hands

Urban problems
litter
parking space
potholes
queues
roadworks
security checks
thieves
to go through red lights
to honk
traffic jams

Rules and regulations
dog owners
fine
lifeguard
to fasten
to clean up after
to refrain from
to tow away
trespasser

Unit 4

School life
badly paid teachers
career counselling
discipline problems
extracurricular activities
one-on-one tutoring
overcrowded classrooms
report
schedule
to behave badly
to cheat in exams
to do the homework
to do well (in school)
to fail a test
to get a low / high mark
to get kicked out of class
to make mistakes
to take a test
tuition fees

University life
certificate
course
degree
graduate
scholarship
to drop out of uni
to get into (medical) school
to enrol

Other words
autism
bribe
deadline
gifted
illiterate
IQ (intelligence quotient)
learning disability
to learn by heart
to procrastinate
to skip
trouble sleeping

Unit 5

Money and shopping
bargain
credit card statement
monthly instalments
shopaholic
shopping sprees
to save money
window shopping

British money
a fiver
a grand
a quid
a tenner

Word formation
ability
actually
apparently
appearance
enjoyment
fitness
freaky
generalise
gorgeous
purify
rejuvenate
remarkable
seriously
shockingly
useless

Other words
aisles
beggar
charity
checkout
gadgets
to donate
to get into debt
to own the bank

Unit 6

TV genres and expressions

billboards
cartoons
chat shows
documentaries
dubbed
game shows
live gigs
medical drama
reality TV
reviews
season
sitcoms
soap operas
sporting events
stand-up comedy
subtitles
the news
to be addicted to
to subscribe to

***Turn* phrases**

to take turns
to turn into
to turn out
to turn up

Films and videos

best-selling
cast
clips
filmmaker
prequel
role
script
sequel
to be nominated
to be set in
to shoot
to star
trilogy
visual effects

Other words

accent
can't stand
composer
views

Unit 7

Car parts

accelerator
boot
bonnet
brake
clutch
engine
steering wheel
tyres
windscreen
wipers

Phrasal verbs

break down
slow down
switch off
turn down
turn off

Operating machines

check
click
plug
push
scroll
set
unplug

Other words

bugs
carrier
launch
warranty

Unit 8

Appearance

cheeks
chin
dark circles
eyelashes
hair
lips
skin
wrinkles

Phrasal verbs

cut down on
cut out
put on
stick to
take up
work out

Furniture

bedside table
blanket / duvet
floor
lamp
pillow
rug
sheet
wall

Unit 9

Crime and punishment

acquit
be arrested
bribery
burglary
charge with
convict
credit card fraud
drug dealing
fine
kidnapping
murder
(music) piracy
release
robbery
send to jail
sentence
take to court
tax evasion
theft

Careers for the future

3D printing engineers
book-to-app converters
nanomedics
privacy manager

Other words

captive
carry out
gang
shoot
spread
targeted
taxpayer
threat
warnings

Unit 10

Moods

bossy
cool as a cucumber
grumpy
moody
pet hates
short-tempered
to be in a good mood
to bite your nails
to get fed up with
to scratch
to swear
to take a deep breath
to yell at

Phrasal verbs

to boss sb around
to bring sb down
to come down with sth
to lift sb up
to look up sth
to phase sb / sth out
to put off sth
to put sb down
to stick to sth
to work sth out

Other words

critical
emotional support
payback plan
tough

Richmond

58 St Aldates
Oxford
OX1 1ST
United Kingdom
© 2015, Santillana Educación, S.L. / Richmond

ISBN: 978-84-668-2196-4
Printed in Brazil
D.L.

Log&Print Gráfica e Logística S.A.
Lote: 769515
Código: 12101831

No unauthorised photocopying.

All rights reserved. No part of this book may be reproduced, stored in a retrieval system or transmitted in any form by any means, electronic, mechanical, photocopying, recording or otherwise, without the prior permission in writing of the Publisher.

Richmond publications may contain links to third party websites. We have no control over the content of these websites, which may change frequently, and we are not responsible for the content or the way it may be used with our materials. Teachers and students are advised to exercise discretion when assessing links.

Publishers: *Ruth Goodman, Sandra Possas*
Content Development: *Paul Seligson*
ID Café and Grammar section: *Pamela Vittorio*
Editors: *Jennifer Wise, Eduardo Trindade, Tom Abraham*
Assistant Editors: *Olivia McGrath, Ed Prosser, Sarah Pollard, Cristiana Cesar, Nathália Horvath*
Art Coordinator: *Christiane Borin*
Art Editor: *Raquel Buim*
Project and Cover Design: *Raquel Buim*
Design Manager: *Lorna Heaslip*
Layout: *HL Studios, Select Editoração*
Artwork: *Gisele A. Rocha, Odair Faléco*
Digital Content: *Jennifer Wise, Jemma Hillyer, Luke Baxter*
Illustrations: *Alexandre Matos, Rico*

Photos: Poznyakov/Shutterstock, 04; File404/Shutterstock, 04; IQoncept/Shutterstock, 04; Maria Taglienti-Molinari/Archive Photos/Getty Images, 06; Thinkstock/Getty Images, 06; Thinkstock/Getty Images, 06; Thinkstock/Getty Images, 06; Preto Perola/Shutterstock, 06; Thinkstock/Getty Images, 07; Thinkstock/Getty Images, 07; Thinkstock/Getty Images, 07; Thinkstock/Getty Images, 07; Thinkstock/Getty Images, 07; Thinkstock/Getty Images, 07; Thinkstock/Getty Images, 07; Edhar/Shutterstock, 07; Jeffrey Blackler/Alamy/Glowimages, 09; Betsie Van der Meer/Stone/Getty Images, 10; Thinkstock/Getty Images, 13; Thinkstock/Getty Images, 14; Zurijeta/Shutterstock, 14; Thinkstock/Getty Images, 14; Aaron Amat/Shutterstock, 14; Jess Yu/Shutterstock, 14; TalyaPhoto/Shutterstock, 16; Galina Mikhalishina/Shutterstock, 16; Thinkstock/Getty Images, 17; Pkchai/Shutterstock, 17; Zurijeta/Shutterstock, 17; Thinkstock/Getty Images, 17; Goodluz/Shutterstock, 17; Sam Edwards/OJO Images/Getty Images, 19; Thomas Barwick/Digital Vision/Getty Images, 22; www.CartoonStock.com, 24; Thinkstock/Getty Images, 27; Tim Hawley/Photographer's Choice/Getty Images, 27; Pidjoe/E+/Getty Images, 27; ZQFotography/Shutterstock, 27; Ollyy/Shutterstock, 27; Reproduction, 29; Frank Carrol/NBCUniversal/Getty Images, 32; Christina Radish/Redferns/Getty Images, 32; SGranitz/WireImage/Getty Images, 32; Barry King/WireImage/Getty Images, 32; Daniel Boczarski/Redferns/Getty Images, 32; Lester Cohen/WireImage/Getty Images, 32; Brad Barket/Shutterstock, 34; Thinkstock/Getty Images, 34; Aaron Amat/Shutterstock, 34; Thinkstock/Getty Images, 34; Emese Benko/ASAblanca/Getty Images, 34; John Sturrock/Alamy/Glowimages, 34; Thinkstock/Getty Images, 35; Gravicapa/Shutterstock, 36; Hill Street Studios/Blend Images/Getty Images, 37; Thinkstock/Getty Images, 37; Robin Skjoldborg/Cultura/Getty Images, 39; Khz/Shutterstock, 39; Dundanim/Shutterstock, 39; Fly_dragonfly/Shutterstock, 39; Voronin76/Shutterstock, 39; Tara Moore/Taxi/Getty Images, 39; Bambu Productions/The Image Bank/Getty Images, 39; Wavebreakmedia/Shutterstock, 40; Jessica Peterson/Tetra images/Getty Images, 41; Levent Konuk/Shutterstock, 41; Gorbelabda/Shutterstock, 41; Popperfoto/Getty Images, 44; Imagebroker/Alamy/Glowimages, 44; Thinkstock/Getty Images, 46; ColorBlind Images/Iconica/Getty Images, 48; Brian A. Jackson/Shutterstock, 48; Philip J. Brittan/Photonica/Getty Images, 48; Reproduction, 51.

Cover Photo: Andresr/Shutterstock, Peter Cade/Iconica/Getty Images, U. Belhaeuser/ScienceFoto/Getty Images, Thinkstock/Getty Images, Michael Peuckert/Imagebroker/Alamy/Other Images.

Videos: My Damn Channel, 6; Geobeats, 15.

Adapted texts: Top 10 Troubled Genius Films/TIME, 23; 10 ways to break free shopping addiction/NBCnews, 24; Why Women Love to Shop/ABCNews, 28; The way they hook us – for 13 hours straight/Newsweek, 29; 8 lies men tell women/e-datefinder, 35; Funny Support Calls/Guy-sports, 37; 8 most unusual weight loss diets from around the world/Tripbaseblog, 39.

We would like to thank the following reviewers for their valuable feedback, which has made *English ID* possible: Adriana Rupp, Ana Beatriz Medeiros de Souza, Brian Lawrence Kilkenny, Clara Haddad, Denise Almeida, Deyvis Sánchez, Diva Maria Abalada Ghetti, Elisabeth Blom, Frank Lício Couto, Henrick Oprea, Isabela de Freitas Villas Boas, José David Ramos Solano, José Olavo Amorin, Juliana Tavares, Kathleen M. Johnson Scholl, Kátia Andréa da Silva Falcomer, Lilian Leventhal, Louise Potter, Luzia Colferai Araujo, Lycia Lourenço Lacerda, Maria Cecília Pérez Gamboa, Maria Luiza Guimarães Carmo, Maria Rute Leal, Mauro Vieira, Pamela Vittorio, René F. Valdívia, Ronaldo Mangueira Lima Junior, Silvana Sanini, Sueli Monteiro, Suzy Teixeira de Almeida, Thais Musa.

Paul Seligson would like to express his incalculable gratitude to all his family, friends, fellow teachers, ex-students, co-authors and the entire Richmond team, without whom *ID* could never have happened. A special thank you to Camila for all her input and support throughout all four levels.

The Publisher has made every effort to trace the owner of copyright material; however, the Publisher will correct any involuntary omission at the earliest opportunity.